THE BLUE CONTINENT

THE
Blue Continent

FOLCO QUILICI

*Illustrated with 26 photographs in colour
and 35 in black and white taken by the author
in collaboration with Viorgio Ravelli*

WEIDENFELD AND NICOLSON
7 Cork Street, London W.1

First published in Great Britain 1954

PRINTED IN GREAT BRITAIN BY
EBENEZER BAYLIS AND SON, LTD., THE
TRINITY PRESS, WORCESTER, AND LONDON

IV

to Bruno Vailati

Contents

Colour illustrations between pages 6 and 7, 54 and 55, 102 and 103.
Black and white illustrations between pages 22 and 23, 70 and 71, 118 and 119

I

Trials above and below

I WAS about eighty feet under water with my camera off the coast of Ponza, a rocky little island which lies between the mainland of Italy and Sardinia, when I heard a bicycle bell. Turning around quickly, I saw Professor Francesco Baschieri Salvadori crouching with an underwater gun, on the butt of which a tinkling object gave out dull musical tones. A few moment later, to my amazement, I saw a school of silver mullets buzzing closer and closer around him at every clang of the bell, until finally one was caught.

The professor had noted on previous dives that these fish seemed to be attracted by certain metallic sounds from his gun, so he had decided to summon them with a bell. On that day I learned how easy it was to film these ordinarily diffident and shy fish.

This story among hundreds gives some idea of why Professor Baschieri, better known as Cecco, was leader of the scientific group of the Italian National Underwater Expedition, which was then undergoing extensive tests and preliminary experiments at Ponza before leaving for its main theatre of exploration, the Red Sea. Cecco had been a law student when he decided that he preferred butterflies, ants, and all things that crawled, squirmed, and swam. He had for several years carried out important underwater research for the Institute of Zoology, and knew fish as one knows one's intimate friends—their vanities and foibles, whims and tricks. A 121-pound package of exuberance, wit, and noise, Cecco's resounding rages were colourful, and his conversation was peppered with lewd expressions in a style uniquely his own.

Raimondo Bucher, chief of the sports group, was quite different. Silent, taciturn, stubbornly training his body for great feats, tenaciously perfecting and testing his equipment, this Italian champion of underwater hunters, holder of the World Free-Body Diving Record, was the kind that grew on you during the long siege of an expedition. But you should meet these people under water.

At Ponza, I filmed Bucher in action for the first time. After slipping into the sea with my camera, I waited while he completed his preparations in his usual meticulous manner. Then he dived and I began to follow him. He descended slowly, aquatically perfect, paddling his fins with a very precise rhythm. On his right a rocky peak rose from some invisible depth, and Bucher stopped near it, about fifty feet down.

A huge cernia, or grouper, appeared, intrigued, and stopped in a head-down position a short distance from Raimondo. This is the typical attitude of observation of the cernia, with only its lateral fins moving and its big mouth slightly open. Bucher approached him cautiously, but, before he could fire, the fish glided toward the bottom with a quick flick of his powerful tail.

Bucher was immediately transformed from a slow and cautious hunter into a speedily flashing assailant. His muscles flexed, and I saw him crouching and springing behind his prey, beating the fins with a force almost as great as that of the splendid tail of the cernia. He disappeared in the blue-green depths at about eighty feet.

I surfaced, but continued to peer toward the bottom. Several seconds passed before Raimondo reappeared, grasping the huge cernia by his fingers in the creature's eyes. He had chased it down almost a hundred feet, shot it, and brought it to the surface as unconcerned as if he had walked round the block. I began to feel encouraged about the kind of pictures I would be able to bring back from the Red Sea, with an aquatic artist like this as a star performer.

I was director of the documentary group, with two assistants. Giorgio Ravelli was an old friend, an able deep-sea enthusiast, and an engineer who specialized in the construction of submarine apparatus such as protective cases for still and moving-picture cameras, flash bulbs, lighting installations, thermocolourmeters, special harpoons, and so on.

The second photographer was Masino Manunza, whom I had never met until one day at Ponza when I was down about fifty feet with an auto-respirator. I had taken moving pictures of a beautiful cernia, then put my camera on the sand floor and shot the cernia with an underwater gun. According to its custom, the big fish had immediately threaded its way into a deep chasm in the rocks.

Pulling and tugging in every direction on the arrow of the gun, I was toiling like mad to extract the cernia from the cave. When I least expected it, I heard a voice with a rather nasal twang: 'Try the hook!'

I was so shocked at hearing a voice fifty feet down that I turned to say, 'Oh, thanks,' to the newcomer before realising where I was. Then I saw a figure thrashing about and offering me a stick of wood with a curved hook. Behind the mask were two little eyes, round, sly, and benevolent at the same time, full of laughter.

'I am Masino,' announced the nasal voice.

I made appropriate gestures of raising my hat and shaking his hand, and mentally replied, 'How do you do. I'm Quilici.' And so began our long friendship.

Three minutes later a cernia lay flopping on the bottom of the boat. We took off our auto-respirators, and I learned the secret of the underwater voice. Masino had a mouthpiece made

3

of a kind of waterproof membrane which permitted him to speak beneath the sea. By the time we sat down that evening to a dish of boiled cernia, I knew that he would be a valued collaborator as well as a friend.

At Ponza we were busy not only testing equipment and getting ourselves in shape, but learning to live and work together as a team, or rather three teams consisting of four scientists, four sportsmen, and three documentarians. Bruno Vailati, dynamic, optimistic, energetic, was the organiser and leader of the whole expedition and part of the scientific group, along with Luigi Stuart Tovini and Gianni Roghi working under Cecco Baschieri. In Raimondo Bucher's sports group was his wife Enza, along with Silverio Zecca and Alberto Grazioli, who was also the expedition's doctor. At the last moment a young lady, Priscilla Hastings, joined the scientific group to make sketches and keep records of specimens.

We lived together in a fisherman's house on a cliff, and dived together in the waters below, testing the equipment to which we would entrust our lives and with which we hoped to make significant discoveries.

First, there were the respirators. We were all accustomed to auto-respirators, in which the expelled breath is regenerated each time, more or less on the principle of the gas mask, by passing through caustic soda or calcified lime in a bag worn on the chest. For our work in the Red Sea we would use not only these, but also air respirators, or aqualungs, with two little tanks of compressed air carried on the back, a pressure reducer, and two rubber tubes leading to the mouth. With these, because of their ability to equalise outside pressures, we could descend without any fear almost two hundred feet and remain about twenty minutes. Note the 'without fear'—a most important point. Using the aqualung there is no danger of fainting spells, auto-intoxication, or lung disturbances, which may sometimes occur with the auto-respirator. There is fresh new air entering the

4

lungs all the time. But twenty minutes is usually its limit, especially at great depths. The auto-respirator is good for two hours, even though we cannot go down nearly so far with it.

Day after day we dived and paddled to test different types of fins. Some wanted rigid fins, others flexible soft fins, but we all agreed on a type quite different from those commonly used in Italy. They cover the entire foot, including the heel—an important protection against the long thorns found almost everywhere in the sea.

Our armament sounded like something dreamed up between an army ordnance expert and an Indian of the Amazon jungles— some of it very modern and the rest, things used by savages. We had both jet-propulsion guns and curare-poisoned harpoons.

The jet-propulsion gun, which may in time become the principal weapon of the future inhabitants of the Blue Continent, deserves its name, for its great power is exerted by gas pressure from a small tank in the butt. An arrow which is hollow for most of its length is inserted in the barrel of the gun. When one presses the trigger, the arrow is blasted out by the high-pressure gas. It gains greater and greater speed as it travels, for the gas contained in its hollow interior discharges itself from the rear, advancing the projectile according to the rules of jet propulsion and leaving behind a silver streak of little bubbles.

The curare harpoon pierces the body of a fish, after which two small wings open and break a vial containing curare, which quickly acts to render the stricken beast harmless, and then kills it.

We had many other guns to try out, too, including one constructed by Bucher which has a super-compressed spring of such power that a special jack was needed to wind it by hand. In order to pierce the skin of a shark, guns must throw the spear and harpoon with tremendous force, and we had to have weapons more powerful than those customarily used in undersea hunting.

5

The training and testing period finally ended, and we all hurried back to the city to put our affairs in order and get ready for the journey to the Red Sea. Then came delays, and more delays—apparently the inevitable hazard of all expeditions. The principal problem was financial. Vailati had figured that the cost of the expedition would be covered by public and private subscriptions—and these came in with some difficulty. The Goggler Club of Milan, the largest Italian underwater sports society, was sponsoring the expedition. To its own contribution, the club added the proceeds of a film festival of international underwater documentaries, which was organised with great success during the summer at the principal swimming resorts. But we needed much more. Raimondo Bucher volunteered to try a spectacular exploit in order to get publicity for the expedition. He would undertake a public attempt to break the skin-diving record of 115 feet!

The announcement was made, the representatives of the press swarmed around like flies, and we all gathered together in a small boat that carried us out to the spot chosen for the great event. Rain poured down steadily, and a chilling wind tossed the water into choppy waves that rocked the boat. Several newspapermen and photographers lost interest in sport and spent some time leaning over the rail, their faces almost as green as the tilting waters round them. Even Raimondo felt a bit uneasy at the pit of his stomach—not a very encouraging sign. Despite cold and rain and seasickness, however, he was determined to go ahead. Public attention had been focused on his attempt, and he wanted to take full advantage of it.

Bucher was in wonderful condition and quite confident. We all knew that he could set the record under good conditions. But now? If he succeeded, he would give invaluable aid to the expedition. But if he failed, perhaps the expedition would lose prestige, and reduce our chances of raising funds even further.

6

The author, with his camera, preparing to dive, and Giorgio Ravelli, sitting in the boat. Note the two types of underwater respirator — the aqualung, with compressed air in yellow tanks worn on the back, good for short periods at depths up to two hundred feet; and the autorespirator, using oxygen and sodium hydroxide, worn on the chest and permitting submersion up to three hours, but dangerous at more than eighty feet.

The 135-ton Formica, which carried the members of the National Underwater Expedition to the Blue Continent.

Three expedition members in the waters of the Coral Barrier of Shadwan, Egypt. Raimondo Bucher, world's record holder for the free-body dive, carries the gun. Behind him are Silverio Zecca and the expeditions's leader, Bruno Vailati.

A hunter nearing the surface with his catch, a red cherna, or grouper, weighing about fifty pounds.

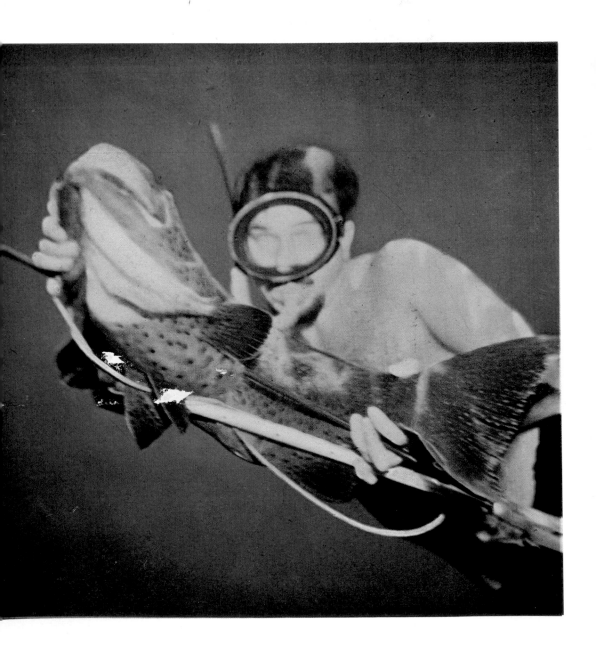

Some small, colorful inhabitants of the Blue Continent
— a butterfly fish and a catapult fish, swimming near
coral formations of « brain » Madrepore.

Cooking some fish that « escaped » the expedition's Scientific Group: Priscilla Hastings, young English artist, assisting Professor Baschieri; the Professor himself; Folco Quilici; a native helper; at extreme left, Gianni Roghi.

Along the shore of Gundabilu, one of the volcanic islands of the Dahlack Archipelago in the Red Sea.

Enza Bucher swims through the super-structure of a scuttled Italian ship, now covered with bright sponges, Madrepore, and Alcyonaria.

The newspapermen seemed sceptical but curious. They bombarded me with questions.

'What are you going to do with this thing here?' a fat journalist asked me, pointing to my movie camera in its big watertight case.

'I'm going down to film Bucher's attempt.'

'And these things—what are they?'

'Auto-respirators,' I explained. 'One for me; one for a friend of Bucher's, Mercante, who will be a hundred feet down; one for the official judge; and one for Vailati, who will be at the bottom to help Bucher if necessary.'

One man asked me what I thought of the letter Bucher had received from a German doctor advising him against exceeding a hundred feet. Beyond that depth, he said, grave damage might occur—at least a lung hæmorrhage. But I had seen Raimondo fishing below a hundred feet several times, and he had always returned lively and gay. I think scientists sometimes set absolute limits that apply only to ordinary human beings, not to an exceptional man like Bucher.

'But five atmosphere-strata of water!' one man protested. 'At thirty-three feet atmospheric pressure is doubled, at sixty-six tripled, and so on. His body will have to support a weight of forty tons at every point on its surface. It's madness!' I looked at the man and decided from his pale face and thick eyeglasses that he was the correspondent of a leftist newspaper. I was saved from answering by a big wave that threw us against the rails. When we all reorganised ourselves, I found myself in the centre of a different group.

'What about his ears?' a man asked.

He would put a clamp on his nose. This would close the Eustachian tubes connecting the nose and ears, creating pressure on the internal side of the eardrums. Thus as the external pressure increased, so would the internal. The balanced pressure would protect the eardrums.

7

'But what will he wear?' interrupted a man who was obviously late in gathering his facts and had failed to read even our announcement.

'Fins, a mask, a nose clamp, webbed gloves, and a gun—the customary apparel of the underwater hunter.'

'Nothing else?' And he shivered, despite his greatcoat and scarf.

'Judging from the weather,' I said, 'I think he should also get himself an umbrella.' This sarcasm failed to silence them.

'Personally, how do you think he will do?'

'I am certain he will succeed,' I announced. 'No doubt of it!'

But I knew I was lying, so I turned to prepare once more the waterproof case for my camera. There had already been difficulties, delays, and such things tell on the morale of a competitor under great strain. First, the crew had been unable to lower a small boat into the water because of the waves. Then it had taken some time to find the right spot for lowering the 150-foot cable. It had to reach to the bottom, where Vailati would station himself. Along it were attached corks at different levels, properly marked. They had to be fixed lightly so that Bucher could snatch and bring to the surface the one at his lowest point. Some of these corks came loose and had to be attached again. But finally everything was ready.

'Get in line, all in line!' shouted a photographer, who wanted us all to undress together—Raimondo and those going into the water with him.

We started to peel off clothing down to our bathing suits. How cold it was! The bystanders, warmly dressed, grew pale as they watched us, pulled on gloves, wrapped scarves tightly round their necks. I looked at Mercante and watched the raindrops roll over the goose pimples that covered his skin. Not even the heat of a hundred flash bulbs warmed us, and we all complained loudly about the cold.

But we had no real complaints. We were actually proud to be helping Bucher at this moment.

8

At one o'clock we were in the water. Then a wave carried the boat too far away, and we waited while it manœuvred into place. Vailati, on his way down, became entangled in the cable with corks, two corks came loose and bobbed to the surface. We had to go down to attach them once more; the judge had to go down too to see that all was in order. Then we all boarded the boat, and sat there shivering, until everything was ready again.

Just before three o'clock we were all in position—Vailati at the bottom, Mercante at one hundred feet, I at sixty-five feet. I planned to shoot a general panorama of the scene with my camera, catching him from the moment he dived and following him from the surface until he disappeared into the deep blue below. Since I could not shoot with colour film below a certain limit, Vailati would capture the historic moment with a photoflash.

Looking up, I saw Raimondo's body break the surface of the water. In an instant he flashed by me, overcoming the wall of water by the powerful blows of his fins. Like an arrow he plunged downwards and I saw Mercante leave his post at one hundred feet to follow the diver, according to plan. At 110 feet, close to the record, Raimondo put his hands to his head and stopped pumping with his feet. Then, with a sudden lunge, he straightened up and pointed toward the surface, giving up his attempt even though he had been so very close to breaking the record.

We all surfaced to find out what was wrong. Nothing serious. His mask had slipped slightly, allowing water to seep inside and cut off his visibility.

We all had to rest before Bucher tried again, and I wondered how his spirits could hold up under this series of demoralising setbacks. The cold water had numbed the muscles on whose flexibility he depended, and the pitching of the boat continued to upset his stomach. But he would not declare himself beaten.

9

The rest of us changed our respirators and tried to warm ourselves a little. At three-fifteen, Raimondo got to his feet and said he was ready. Into the water we went, and Vailati went down to see that all was in order. He surfaced with the good news that the water, which had been rather muddy, was now much clearer below the sixty-five feet level. Raimondo made a shallow dive and surfaced beside us at the buoy. We dived to our positions, and were scarcely in place when I saw Bucher's body break the surface. A shadow skimmed past me and I trained my camera on it. The sight of the confident power of his strokes renewed my lost confidence. When he disappeared below I surfaced and waited. A second went by, another second. I heard the voice of a radio-commentator on the boat. 'Still he hasn't appeared. One minute. . . . One minute ten seconds. . . . One minute fifteen seconds. . . . HERE HE IS!'

Raimondo's head bobbed to the surface, and he tossed a small cork happily in the air. I swam to retrieve it and heard him cry, 'Thirty-nine metres!'

A hundred and twenty-eight feet! A new world record.

Bucher climbed up on the boat, with the rest of us behind him. Suddenly he staggered slightly, and I had to support him. But it was only a momentary collapse; at extreme depths, the peripheral circulation of the blood ceases. When one rises rapidly to the surface, the abrupt change in pressure causes the blood to flow back into the peripheral blood vessels, bringing sudden weakness and dizziness.

Raimondo was himself again in time to hear the applause from everyone on the boat and his wife Enza's cries of joy.

The press made a terrific fuss about the new record. *Life* magazine devoted two pages to the man who had gone down to 128 feet in only a bathing suit. The news echoed round the world and people became very interested in the National Underwater Expedition to the Red Sea.

The Italian Olympics Committee made a contribution, so did the Superior Council of Research, with a promise of further help. Many individuals helped us, and institutions and corporations contributed much-needed equipment. Professor Baschieri received scientific instruments from the University of Rome. Food companies gave us provisions and mineral water. And finally *Societa Anonima Lavorazioni Varie Apparecchi di Salvataggio* of Rome supplied everything we needed in the way of auto-respirators, fins, and masks that we had chosen during our tests and trials.

With all this help, the expedition was on its way.

2

Our first coral jungle

EVERYTHING takes longer than you expect, especially the things you want most. It was 27 December before we left, instead of the end of September. Even when everything else was fixed up, we had trouble finding the right ship that would carry us to the Red Sea and serve as our floating base. Promises and refusals of ships from the Navy alternated with telephone calls to Bruno Vailati, who was kept busy receiving, examining, and rejecting the proposals of shipbuilders and private owners.

Finally everyone decided to cut short the promises and suggestions and find an adaptable vessel. Vailati, Masino, and Baschieri set out in our little utility car to find a ship. Some time later they telegraphed that they had found something useful at Civitavecchia—a small motor-ship that had transported Pecorino cheese from Sardinia to Italy for six years. We all rushed down to see it.

The *Formica* was a small ship—135 tons, 93 feet long, 23 feet wide, with a motor capable of pushing the vessel along at the breath-taking speed of seven miles per hour. But it looked comfortable, and was clean and trim, with a slender, sure line and a bell-prow. It made a favourable impression on us as it rode at anchor under the immense stern of the transatlantic liner, *Saturnia*.

There was a good crew of four: Captain Solari, a big strong man with black eyes and a booming voice (the way he wore his peaked cap reminded me of Walt Disney's 'Old Sea Wolf');

the boatswain Mollo, who was a Tuscan, nervous and usually bad tempered; Mauro, the mechanic, young and pleasant and always laughing; and finally Giuseppe (called 'Peppe'), a comic fellow, one of whose duties was slowly poisoning us, for he was the cook.

Apart from the crew's quarters, there was a space divided into two compartments with four bunks, two on each side in double-decker fashion—in an area so small that it would not even have been acceptable as a mountain hideout. Since this was not enough room for us, an extra cabin with eight places had to be constructed on the deck.

The day after Christmas we all gathered in Naples, where the *Formica* awaited us, for our departure. We looked over the little machine room and the wheelhouse, where each of us would take turns working in order to relieve the crew. We tried out our vibrating bunks that measured about a foot less than we did and were built of six parallel planks of wood. But we cheerfully tacked up good-luck mascots and photographs, and made ourselves at home.

One truck arrived with crude oil, another with an icebox, then several more with cases of supplies. We sorted them into different categories—sports, photographic, scientific, and alimentary—and stowed them away neatly along the walls of the hold. From the main hatch we could go down easily and get any of the stores we needed.

Until the last moment of departure, journalists and photographers were crawling over the boat, peering in all the holes, climbing on the rigging, flashing bulbs in our faces, and making Baschieri quake for fear of seeing his fragile and precious aquariums shattered. Finally, at six o'clock in the morning on the twenty-seventh, the *Formica* snorted a blast on its whistle, and we heard for the first time the monotonous rumbling of the motor that would accompany us for many months like a perpetually snoring companion.

13

After waiting so long, we were glad to watch the land disappear behind us. But the weather decided to delay us further, and an angry sea forced us into the port of Capri. There we sat for seven long days, feeling a little silly at only having gone such a short distance after our long preparations. At the end of this time, although the barometer still warned us to be careful, we took heart from a bright moon and a calm sea, and set forth.

For two days all went well. Then the storm struck again. It did not make us feel any better to learn much later that during those stormy two weeks of our trip to Port Said the transatlantic liner *Champollion* had been wrecked on the coast of Libya and an American liberty ship split off Livorno. Through one storm after another we made our way to Greece, passed through the canal of Corinth, and headed towards Crete, with the help of a hurricane at our stern.

At the beginning of the final leap to Egypt, the weather was fine again, but then Neptune decided that we were getting too close to our goal and lashed out with even greater fury. The *Formica* plunged down the side of one wave, wallowed uncertainly for a moment between two walls of water, then panted up the steep hill of the next wave, all the time shaking and quivering. In the extra cabin, the water took over the lower berths as if it belonged there, and four people, four boxes, four suitcases, and one dog crowded into two upper berths. Then the rains began, making the upper berths uninhabitable and, worse still, reducing visibility almost to zero. As a result we almost smashed into a tanker that suddenly crossed our bow. Mollo, who was at the wheel, put the *Formica* into a sharp turn, which made us liable to be overturned in the trough of the waves.

But we managed to keep going, and after a while the seas calmed down slightly, and turned yellow. We realised we had met the waters of the Nile. Congratulating the crew and ourselves, we sailed into the Nile estuary, made our way under the sterns of many great ships, and tied up at a pier in Port Said, amid the catcalls of sailors in Danish, English, German, and many other languages. They were particularly amused at Enza Bucher, who was busy on deck hanging out a long-delayed wash.

We spent one day in the town, and were entertained at dinner by the Italian Consul and colony, and we acted like cannibals after two weeks of seasickness and tinned food. Then we slipped into the marvellous liquid path of the Suez Canal, and on the morning of 18 January saw the first waves of the Red Sea lapping against the prow of the *Formica*.

Why did we choose the Red Sea? There were many reasons. A tropical sea provides the most interesting study because the higher temperature of its waters produces a vigorous fauna and flora, an abundance of specimens of all kinds. In warmer waters, also, men can stay immersed much longer—although the water at great depths is very cold even in the Red Sea. Since the Red Sea is connected with the Mediterranean on one side—and through this sea with the Atlantic—and with the Indian and Pacific Oceans on the other side, it contains forms of life common to all of these masses of water.

The Red Sea, however, is considered the most dangerous in the world because of its superabundance of man-eating fish. But we were looking for sharks, not with any silly idea of being heroic, but in order to study them more thoroughly than they had ever been studied before. Many contradictory stories have been told about sharks, and we had our own ideas about them. We hoped to show, if we all returned home safe and sound, that the inhabitants of the Blue Continent were no more dangerous to men under water than the ordinary hazards and traffic accidents of everyday life are to men on land.

We looked down at these long-sought waters that we should soon explore and, although our ultimate goal was far to the south, we were eager to slip down below and see what the place looked like. But for a time we moved ahead slowly, passing many low rocky islands of the sort that make the Red Sea the most perilous to navigation in the world. Each consisted of a crown of dry rock lying above layers of stratified coral and madrepore. Beyond the visible rock, the layers stretched out for some distance, only ten or twelve feet below the surface of the water, but almost invisible; a terrible trap for unwary ships that ventured too near. Because of such shoals, the Red Sea is dotted by beacons that throw rays of light to the hundreds of ships that use this busy route linking East and West.

We were interested because we knew that on and around such shoals we would perform a great deal of our work, for here lay the headquarters of tropical underwater life. From the deep abyss arose these formations, building evil castles, fortifications, spires, towers, and pinnacles amidst which swim the citizens of the deep. Sometimes their crests reached above the surface; sometimes they lurked just below. We would find many as far down as we could dive.

We saw the light of the beacon on the island of Shadwan shortly after midnight and anchored near it about three a.m. As dawn came, we all stared at this example of nature's absent-mindedness. From the point of view of aridity and squalor, we were to see much worse in the future, but this was our first sight of such barrenness, and we were terrified. Nature, usually so lavishly generous, had here placed an island twice as large as Capri, consisting only of cones of rock and pink sand. When people say 'not a blade of grass', they must mean Shadwan. In the iciest regions of the North or in the driest deserts, there is always some vegetation. Even on Mars, according to scientists, there is lichen. On Shadwan—no.

We slipped into our diving equipment and let ourselves down nto the water. As we swam toward the island, the head of the madreporic shoals, the impression of complete barrenness stayed with us. But when we left the ordinary world and began our trip down into the Blue Continent, the unbelievably fabulous spectacle that greeted us seemed like a peace offering to compensate for Shadwan. From the impenetrable blue of the marine depths, the coral barrier rose toward the surface in an infinite variety of blues. It had a multitude of points, ravines, elbows, and recesses—like the stumps of very old, enormous oaks—that burst forth in all directions with a violence that was almost aggressive, with a richness and fantasy beyond imagination.

Now we were all under water, swimming amidst hundreds of different species of fish, between the long arms of coral which were first pink, then purple, then yellow, among the madreporic formations of many-coloured rococo architecture.

Giorgio and I, armed with two cameras, travelled along the jutting cliffs, moving up and down without effort, pointing out the arbalests, the parrot fish, the nail fish, and other inhabitants of this jungle, all of whom darted about investigating us between nibbles at the madrepore and the coral. The coral and madrepore furnish food for very small fish, the small fish are food for larger ones, and so on—a continuous chain of life and death. Thanks to the sun, this flourishing underwater life was without equal.

For almost two hours, we continued our sightseeing tour, hanging onto the cliffs like alpinists, but as this was the Blue Continent unencumbered by large shores, ropes, and axes. Occasionally we saw endless schools of little spindle-topped, sky-blue fish, as long as one's hand, darting towards the open sea. Dark red, violet-spotted cernias also wandered about, looking at us curiously with two prominent eyes, then slowly disappearing into their inaccessible coves. The only noise that broke the absolute silence of this coral jungle was the mass of air bubbles escaping from our respirators. They chased each other through the many holes, channels, and knots of the madrepore—crossing

the enormous sheets of umbrella-like millipore, which are perforated like sixth-century lace—and made their way noisily and
speedily to the surface.

We were busy making the acquaintance of the coral jungle,
our only contact with the surface a silver chain of bubbles. And
Giorgio, Masino, and I were happily making the first Red Sea
tests of the equipment over which we had laboured so long.
Now we were reaping the rewards of those days and evenings at
Ponza, and afterward, when Giorgio had discarded the old type
of case for movie cameras and designed a new one. He had built
dozens of models, and I had tried them, after which we had
had endless hours of discussion about this or that screw, about its
position half an inch to the right or left, about precise angles
to be used. Giorgio finally made a case, not only containing all
the operational gadgets for adjusting the focus and diaphragm,
but also with a little system of knobs which would permit us to
change the lenses under water, passing quickly from very large
close-ups to fine telescopic shots. Then the entire case was
equipped with wings and stabilisers like an aeroplane so that
it could retain its proper balance in the water.

Giorgio had also made a new waterproof case for our Contax,
so small and simple that it was a pleasure to use, and another
for a large Rolleiflex which enabled it to be focused directly
through the ground glass, even under water, reducing by ninety-
five per cent the possibility of bad focusing. And the Rolleiflex
had a flash, a most important innovation, that would enable us
to bring out the colours in the dark grottos and at great depth.
With it we could conquer the mysterious, impenetrable blue of
the deep sea and pierce its veil to uncover the enchantment that
has been concealed since the creation of the world.

With Masino, I had thrashed out the problems concerned with
colour, only one of which had been overcome by using the flash
bulb at great depths. The photographer who works with colour
film knows that it is not very difficult to use effectively if he has

stillness, time, and enough light. Under water you have none of these essentials. Down on the bottom we would have to take what we could, quickly. There would be no possibility of reloading, no chance to set the scene. Our documentary shots would have to come right the first time. The deeper you go, of course, the more the colours disappear, as the rays of the sun are filtered out by the mass of the blue sea. All the so-called warm colours —red, orange, pink, and yellow—disappear after fifteen or twenty feet, growing dimmer the deeper you go.

We had made a series of tests with filters that would restore some of these lost colours.

We had worked and tested and had been satisfied. But here was the real test—in the Red Sea. Eagerly we tried out all our new tricks and even more eagerly awaited the results. You can see some of them in this book and judge for yourself.

After the first day of diving, we sat long over dinner exchanging our impressions of the Red Sea. We were eager to get on to our base and get to work in earnest. The next morning we headed south again.

I was serving my turn at the wheel, and Cecco Baschieri and the captain were near by, when we saw a sudden breaking of white foam about three hundred feet ahead of us. The map indicated no shoal near this point, but we felt that no map could show every one of these traps, so we kept our eyes open to see if another whitecap appeared, which might mean the breaking of a wave on a half-hidden madreporic bank.

Then the white foam gleamed off to the right, and we realized that it was caused by something moving, something with a large tail and fin.

'A shark! A shark!'

The great fish we had been wanting to see had come out to meet us. Everyone ran to the bow, and a harpoon was quickly made ready. The water was broken again by a violent blow of

the fins, and a thick, shiny, glistening body leapt out of the
water and fell back again with a crash. We saw a triangular
fin and bubbling water. Fins and tails appeared and disappeared. Then, standing erect from the water like a little
metal flag, a long black fin. Around it the water became
muddy from a vast and oily mark of blood that spread over the
surface.

When we arrived at the spot, we found only a piece of a large
fish, which we identified as the remains of a swordfish. Enormous bites had been taken from the body, and blood was gushing
forth. We had seen a dramatic duel between a swordfish and
one or more sharks. We judged that there must have been more
than one shark; one alone could not have eaten so much in a
few seconds. We decided that a group of sharks must have risen
suddenly from the depths, surrounded their succulent prey and,
after a violent fight, overcome and devoured it—no doubt a
battle that was repeated a thousand times a day among the
monsters of the sea.

We were just about to harpoon the remains of the swordfish
and bring it aboard for observation when a shadow came up
very slowly under the keel of the ship. It was one of the victors
coming to see what we were doing with his meal—a dignified
and imposing mackerel shark of very tranquil stature about
fourteen feet long. He swam about two and a half feet below
the surface, gazing with his small, sly eyes at the carcass of the
swordfish. Frightened by our shouts of surprise and enthusiasm,
he sank away under water with a flashing stroke of his tail. We
were hurrying to get our cameras, when one of the seamen cried
out, 'Here it is! Here it is again!'

The shark advanced slowly towards the surface, swaying
slightly as it approached its prey, then it took such a tremendous
bite with such speed and such incredible force that I gave an
involuntary shiver of horror.

Bruno Vailati, hanging over the rail with a harpoon, hurled

it with all his might and struck the shark right in the middle. The steel harpoon, on a hardwood javelin seven feet long and almost three inches thick, transfixed the fish, paralysing it for the fraction of a second. We all held our breath as it twisted slowly round, as if understanding where the danger came from. Turning completely on its back, the shark defiantly opened and closed its mouth twice with majestic slowness, and then with a sudden flashing movement broke the pole in two. Into the blue depths he disappeared, to die in silence and dignity, far from the eyes of man, as befitted the King of the Sea.

A few days later, on the way south, we decided that we should put in at the little port of Cosseir, which we had found on the map, to replenish our water. One morning it appeared suddenly before us out of a fog so thick that the island seemed to be floating just above the sea. It not only looked unreal, but the town near the shore actually was unreal. We all stood and stared.

'It's a mirage,' Gigi Stuart said. 'We've all had sunstroke.'

On the shore, on the pier, on the boats, around the houses, we saw not one living being. Usually when our ship entered any harbour, boats filled with police and customs officials —two things never lacking even in the most microscopic countries of the world—hurried out at once, followed by all sorts of people with things to sell. But at Cosseir there was no sign of life.

We decided to spend some time diving around the beautiful madreporic shoal which we dimly saw a short distance away under the crystalline tops of the waves. Here we met an interesting new species of tropical fish—an example of local tuna (which although huge was smaller than that of the Mediterranean tuna) streaked with purple-blue veins. Flopping about the school of tuna were thousands of little sardines, so thick that we seemed to be immersed in sardines rather than in water. When a tuna approached the sardines, they skipped away with such speed that it was hard to see the surface of the water, for they jumped by the hundreds on top of the waves. Later, this scene was repeated farther south where smaller tuna took the place of the sardines fleeing from larger tuna.

In the sand on the bottom, a short distance from the reef, I saw four or five gasoline tanks that had fallen into the sea. Coming from one tank I saw something that looked like a black rope about seven feet long. The same thing emerged from another tank, and I swam closer to see what these creatures were. Just as I arrived, a beautiful sting ray came out of a tank, rapidly beating its winglike fins and pulling behind it an endless tail. There was a ray in each tank, and within a few minutes, four of them were circling about me, very much disturbed. I hid myself, and shortly the four-winged creatures re-entered their convenient homes to continue their naps.

Meanwhile, Zecca had bagged one of the tuna, which was endowed with such a robust constitution that it put up a strenuous fight even when mortally wounded. Bruno had made a good catch, too—a sea eel. The scientific group was pleased because it was the first specimen that we had seen of the white sea eel, for most of these creatures are blackish, or brown with yellow spots. The white type is found only in the southern part of the Red Sea, so Baschieri claimed it at once for his jar of formalin, despite the protests of some of us who were thinking about lunch.

Ten minutes later we had another specimen for the jar of formalin, a boxfish, one of the most curious creatures I have ever seen. Its body is a sort of hard, rectangular box that looks like a small jewel chest—compact, armoured, and smooth. It doesn't really look like a fish at all, but like a box suspended in the water. When it tries to move, it really looks ridiculous, for it depends on two small fins sticking out of two holes on the front of its body—fins so tiny that they can only move the fish

The calm that precedes the storm . . . the
Mediterranean was troubled by numerous
squalls during our crossing.

Masino Manunza using the special underwater camera which enabled us to record the fauna of the Blue Continent.

The reward of a long wait underwater—a shark feeding.

An angry shark struggles on the end of a harpoon as it is dragged to the surface.

The sucking fish is the shark's faithful companion: it attaches itself by its sucker to the shark's nose or stomach and never leaves it.

Raimondo Bucher swims to the surface after a successful struggle with a shark.

A close up of a brown shark.

A six foot 'black nosed' shark shows his dangerous teeth.

Our seagull mascot, Gregory, stands on the back of a giant ray; beside him lies a recently caught shark.

Forests of Algæ nearly sixty feet down.

laboriously and at a snail's pace. The boxfish is one of the few underwater creatures that swims which is not streamlined. It is not pointed in front or behind. On the flat front of its box are two microscopic eyes and a small hole. On the back there is a sort of bulge, shaped like a lamp, on which is stuck a comically thin tail. With all these handicaps, however, the boxfish has no fear of being eaten by other fish. It is indigestible.

Baschieri happily collected the third specimen—the big firefish (*pteoris volitans*), one of the most poisonous known. An Arab had told us that he had had a sting from the firefish and had suffered so much pain that his friends had had to tie him to the ground to keep him from throwing himself into the sea. Even when they put hot irons on his swollen foot—a common Arab treatment for any ailment—the iron hurt less than the sting of the firefish.

Baschieri had lectured all of us to be careful of the *pteoris volitans* and made such a deep impression on us that we named it the cobra fish, feeling that this name was more appropriate. In the end Baschieri himself was badly stung by the specimen he caught. Luckily Dr. Grazioli had the right kind of medicine to relieve the pain, so Cecco did not suffer like the poor Arab.

It was I who found the cobra fish, incidentally. It is actually very hard to see, as it hides by blending itself perfectly with its surroundings. On top of this, it is really very rare. I was down below, and saw a twig of coral which seemed to have a strange shape. Getting my camera ready to photograph, I saw it move. So I stuck out my foot and gave it a small tap with one of my fins. (I shudder to think about it now.) It headed for the dark, slowly and majestically, waving eight enchanting fins (four on each side) that seemed more like the wings of an ostrich than fins, and a long, light, fanlike tail. It was about four inches long, small in comparison with others we found later, which ran up to twelve and fifteen inches.

23

Suddenly I saw, along the fish's back, a row of stingers, straight as arrows and extremely sharp. Then I knew what I was dealing with and backed away. Keeping my eye on it while surfacing, I called loudly for Baschieri, who came down at once. He was awe-struck at the marvellous sight, but did not behave very prudently. He harpooned it with a needle harpoon, specially made for delicate specimens, but failed to notice that the fish slipped down against his finger before he could take his hand away from the harpoon.

We got back to the boat as quickly as possible, with Baschieri sucking hard at the wound, and the pain mounting every minute. Then came the incision, the injection, and a certain amount of relief, so that our Professor could take some pleasure in his find.

By this time, Cosseir had proved to us that it did contain living people, for a very pleasant Egyptian captain had come aboard, followed by a military entourage. He invited us all to his office, which was a small 'castle' of stone, filled with blackbirds. Before it stood four imposing cannons ('Captured from Napoleon,' he said). He sat at his desk drinking several bottles of Coca-Cola, with three posters of General Neguib looking down on him. He asked many questions about the expedition—in Italian, English, and French. We replied in the same languages and also drank our fill of Coca-Cola. Then he showed us a collection of shells, embalmed oysters, and live pigeons, the last so tame that they were always walking around behind him.

He told us that behind the port there was an industrial centre, a phosphate factory full of Italians. While we were thinking of a way of taking our leave, the director of the factory arrived, having learned of the arrival of an Italian ship.

He was very polite, and we were quite content to go with him to see the industrial centre of 'lost' Italians living in the middle of the low, interminable, deserted coast of Upper Egypt.

Behind the dry and dusty Arab houses, half crumbling from the sun, and under the ruins of a little fort half buried in the sand, there appeared a group of neat buildings surrounded by many green gardens. Alongside a narrow church stood a larger building, the factory—the 'classical' architecture of Italian villages in Africa.

As we looked over the factory and met Italian technicians, we learned that Cosseir was almost exclusively supported by this industrial centre. The country receives water and light from the factory, which is also responsible for its small activity as a port. The more active population works with the Italians, and the children go to the Italian school. The school is headed by a very agreeable teacher from Venice, who, to his great joy and our great interest, showed us the ichthyological collection he had made since his arrival. Thus the apparently dead island of Cosseir turned out to have in fact plenty of life.

We headed south once more, and ran into a gale near the Suakin islands that made us run for Port Sudan. We entered the channel that leads to the city across a maze of little islands and reefs, and passed the great lighthouse of Sanganeb, a steel structure that looked like a parody of the Eiffel Tower.

Hundreds of sea birds fluttered about us, majestic sea hawks, the usual sea gulls, and other fishing birds that closed their wings and plunged like arrows into the water, reappearing a moment later with fish in their beaks. Besides these new acquaintances, we met on shore Procopio, a Greek of incredible circumference, good humoured, with an unimaginable kitchen. From him we collected a dozen postcards of the Fuzzy-Wuzzies, the handsomest warriors in Africa, with their uniform of shields, feathers and lances, and we had a memorable dinner which greatly extended our knowledge of Arab dishes.

South again, in a voyage that seemed twice as long as we had expected. Then we saw a large town in the distance. As we approached, we saw that it stretched out toward the sea on a huge island which was joined to the mainland by a long dike. Two Arab boats with dazzling white triangular sails that nearly touched the water appeared beside us to guide us to land. At nine-thirty on 27 January, the *Formica* was tied to the pier of Massaua, our real goal.

3

Clandestine Diving

THERE was a great deal of traffic on board the *Formica*, with many uniformed officials—police, customs, medical inspectors—investigating, counting, verifying, stamping, discussing, and affixing signatures. We asked for transit visas from the authorities and work permits for the Dahlak Archipelago. The visas were apparently easy, but the work permits were another matter. There had to be a good deal of investigation. It would take a little time.

If for any reason the authorities refused us the permits, we planned to move on to Kamaran, a British island off the coast of Yemen, surrounded by an interesting archipelago. But we preferred to make Massaua our headquarters. We had to have a port properly equipped for the handling of bottles of oxygen and compressed air for respirators and other equipment. We needed space for workshops in which to make repairs, and a base which was handy to Italy so that we could send off exposed films right away. The heat and humidity of the southern Red Sea were death to them, even though they were protected by metal boxes and hygroscopic salts.

The officials left, and we realised that the permits would eventually arrive, but not for several days at least. We tried to make the best of the delay by sightseeing in Massaua and lying in wait to photograph the evening drives of the Negus,

27

Haile Selassie, ruler of the former Italian colony of Eritrea now annexed to Ethiopia.

The sky-blue Cadillac of Haile Selassie moved slowly down the street about six o'clock, preceded by the Imperial Guard in three lemon-coloured jeeps. The Negus sat behind wearing a tall peaked cap covered with gold braid. He acknowledged the salutes of the people with a brief nod. Two reddish fox terriers frisked about on the back seat near him.

He reminded me more of a member of the City Council of a seaside resort to whom crowds of men in shorts and white shirts wave and bow without too much movement for fear of sweating. There was something too intimate and informal about the scene to make one think of an emperor. But it made the Negus seem quite likeable and sympathetic. Even the Italians, who certainly did not welcome the loss of Eritrea to Ethiopia, regarded him with sympathy and spoke of him with admiration.

This was not enough to satisfy us. We had made preparation and waited so long that we were impatient to get to work, make our explorations, gather our information and test our theories.

Just what were these theories? What was the purpose behind the expedition and what did we hope to accomplish? There had been other underwater expeditions, some to the Red Sea. How was our expedition different? In some ways it was not so very different. There had been so little exploration of this new world which was almost a new universe, that most of it remained hidden and unknown, offering fields for scores of expeditions. Like the others, we wanted to learn all we could about everything we came across and record it both thoroughly and carefully. Beyond that, we wanted to concentrate on getting something new. For one thing, we planned to make a long and intensive study of prolonged underwater diving in different localities under different conditions. As part of this aim,

Dr. Grazioli planned to keep daily records, on behalf of the Medical Sports Federation, of the physical and psychological effects of prolonged immersions and of the behaviour of the men who moved and worked in the Blue Continent.

The scientific group's aim was to assemble a vast collection of specimens of every type of marine life, chiefly for the Civic Museum of Zoology of Milan. Every shell, every fish, every plant would add to man's knowledge of the underwater world, a world of such riches that all the farms and factories and mines of the exploited and developed world above the seas could not provide a tenth of the energy, minerals, and foods of this new Continent. The human race, growing by leaps and bounds despite the starvation and undernourishment of two-thirds of its number, needs a new world to explore and develop, a new store-house of sustenance, materials, and power. The surface of the sea is the new frontier across which the enterprising and adven-turous push to-day so that in the future all men can reap the harvests of these limitless acres, an area three times as great as all the land on earth.

We felt that men would have to abandon their old concepts of the sea—as a place to swim, a place to boat and a liquid from which to extract a few fish by dropping lines and nets just below the surface. We wanted men to conquer the depths as they have conquered the air above them—actually a far easier and infinitely more rewarding venture than ascending into the stratosphere. Neither place has enough oxygen, but man's ingenuity has already overcome that handicap. In the strato-sphere there is nothing, but in the deep sea there are millions of living creatures of thousands of varieties, plants nutritious and beautiful, gold and other precious minerals. And everywhere there is beauty—of colour, design, and form. Boys dream of man-made satellites, of spaceships, and space suits in which they can soar upwards unhampered by the pull of gravity. But the explorers of the sea, of the Blue Continent, already have their space suits, in which they drift at ease through their new environment, unfettered by gravity, able to send themselves up or down, forward or backward, with the most casual effort.

The exploration of the new Continent beneath the water, as we planned it, would be thoroughly documented—with still pictures, moving pictures, written descriptions of every important item we found. That was the work of my group. And finally, there was the sports programme. For one thing, the hunting and catching of this group would supply the scientific group with its specimens. But it also had a programme of its own: an attempt to carry out aquatic big-game hunting in ways that had never been tried before. Many men had preceded us in diving among sharks and other dangerous fish, and had proved that they do not attack when one dives. Hans Hass had done it. Cousteau had done it, carrying a stick to push back sharks which approached too close. We planned to carry the study of sharks even further, shooting them to observe if, and when, they recovered their courage, subjecting them to all kinds of stimuli to study their psychology. We wanted to continue the task of removing from sharks their blood-stained halo of superstition and tall tales and replace it with the light of known facts.

These and a dozen other goals lay behind the expedition, and behind our impatience to get on with our work. That is why we listened eagerly to the advice of a few friends who suggested that we could make a clandestine start, if we went about it with discretion and little fuss. Not far away there was a little island called Sceik Said, named after a prophet who was supposed to be buried there. Promising coral reefs lay around it, which we decided to investigate.

We decided not to move the *Formica* or even our small boat. Instead we went to the little island and hired small boats used for ferrying, working almost under the noses of the guards, who seemed chiefly preoccupied with keeping me from walking along the streets of Massaua in a bathing suit, as I had done one hot day.

A great disappointment was in store for us at Sceik Said. The waters were muddy, but not from dirt or sediment. The lack of transparency came from billions of plankton, the tiny one-celled creatures, animal and vegetable, that are the staff of life of all the seas. Most of them are microscopic in size, and they float about in dense clouds. Their presence in such super-abundance meant one good thing, however: there would be plenty of fish about, for plankton furnish the principal food of the ocean to creatures ranging from the sardine to the whale. I have heard that if one took an enormous quantity of plankton and mixed it with the meat of a crayfish or other fish, one would have croquettes which would not only have a high nutritive value but also a delicious flavour.

Clouds of plankton have been given as the reason behind variations in depth readings made by electronic devices that are highly accurate. Even in the same spot readings indicated that the bottom of the sea had risen or fallen in periods corresponding to night and day. Since the bottom obviously stays just where it ought to be, the only reasonable explanation was a cloud of plankton so dense that they reflected the electronic signals like a solid mass. We were able to confirm this hypothesis during our work in the Red Sea, when we noted that the best hours for photography were between seven and nine in the morning, for at nine the cloud of plankton rose and reduced our visibility.

Our first dives were unsatisfactory. For one thing, none of us could help thinking about sharks. Bruno, Bucher and Gigi spoke with unashamed fear of encountering sharks, for everyone we had talked to at Massaua was terrified of them. We would also have felt better at our first meetings with these creatures if we could have seen clearly. Even if the experts said sharks were harmless, we preferred to verify these statements when visibility was good. In a few days, however, we relaxed and even got used ourselves to the muddiness. And then we learned that below thirty or thirty-five feet, the water was much clearer. So down we went.

At Sceik Said there is a famous coral precipice which rises from the bottom in many peaks up to within a few yards of sea level—big and calm and imposing, a huge petrified forest, a living and growing forest continually changing and increasing itself. Like all the rocky reefs in this region it is made of millions of creatures called Coelenterata. Madrepore and coral are not lifeless minerals, but columns constructed by tiny gelatinous animals which give out calcium carbonate—hard and rocky. The scaffold is continually being formed, so that a coral bank or precipice can truly be said to be a living thing. Some of the madrepore, for instance, prove quite conclusively that they are alive when you touch them. One of these is called fire coral by the natives, and gives a strong burn, similar to that of the jellyfish but more painful. Actually, madrepore and jellyfish belong to the same family, despite the fact that they seem so different—one a living skeleton, the most petrified thing in the animal kingdom; and the other the softest and most gelatinous of all.

The madrepore often assume strange forms, and there are about two thousand known species. The most beautiful are those shaped like fungi, opening wide circular umbrellas above a thick central stump. The wide top, as fragile-looking as spun sugar and perforated like old lace, sometimes reaches a diameter of fourteen or fifteen feet, and beneath its shelter are sleepy cernias and other fish. We sometimes hid there in order to watch big fish that came near.

We saw lying on the sands near the bottom of the coral precipice huge 'brain' madrepore, globular and indented by all the convolutions that suggest a human brain. Not far away were stars, thorns, cups, threads, elk-horns, trees—all made of madrepore, some yellow, others violet, light blue, brown and white. On sandy stretches there were small mushrooms, and cups that seemed to be made just to be taken home to serve as ash trays. Silverio, who had a fiancée waiting for him at Ponza, gathered many of these to use as confetti containers on his wedding day.

At Sceik Said we also encountered the rarest type of madrepore —the organ. These were violent-red vertical tubes clinging to rocks or other madrepora and extending to different heights in perfect order. Moving away respectfully, I came upon a vast expanse of the carpet-type of madrepore—wavy, and covered with gay hand-painted designs on its yellow surface.

As if this were not colour enough, we found dozens of plants in the cracks and crevices and along the sides of the varied madreporic formations—sea fans, Alcyonaria, the sea anemone, fluctuating seaweeds of many colours, and whole fields of flowers. On the bottom we saw sponges of every shape, some cadmium yellow and others blood-red, dull grey, and bright orange, holding on to the shirt sleeves of the rocks and coral. At great depths we saw some shaped like cups, twenty to thirty inches across. They are called Neptune's-cup.

The sea anemone, that terrible flesh-eating flower, fascinated me as it does almost every diver in tropical seas. It looks graceful and innocent, with its hundreds of thin tentacles fluctuating slowly in the currents of water. But then I saw a little fish come near, obviously attracted by the appetising substance sent out by the tentacles. Nearer still he swam, and the tentacles reached out, clutched the fish and bore it to the centre of the plant, which closed around it and contracted like a sac of red flesh, until it looked something like a monstrous tomato.

Other fish swam up, famished—little fellows with white dots on their black sides. They stood by, waiting, until the sea anemone reopened and let fall the sucked and inert form of its victim.

Then the spotted parasites pounced upon it to do away with the remains.

Other fish approached, orange-coloured. They were pomacentrids, and they advanced fearlessly toward the outstretched tentacles of the sea anemone. Was this the end of them, too? No. Instead of being seized and enclosed, the two pomacentrids swam into the midst of the waving tentacles and began to clean up the flower industriously. Here I witnessed one of the many examples of mutual service and protection to be found in the sea. I advanced my gun toward the pomacentrids, but they did not flee. Instead, the sea anemone closed them up inside, protecting its 'servants' until the threat was removed. When I withdrew, the flower opened, and the unharmed fish went on with their cleaning task, after which they swam happily away.

Baschieri reported another example of the same sort of thing. He saw a big parrot fish standing still, with its snout in the air and its mouth open. Two small blue fish were busily cleaning the rubbish from its mouth.

Two days later, Bucher and I were amusing ourselves on the bottom, looking for fish subjects to photograph. We met a large sea eel of sinister brown and violet colour, sticking its head out of a hole in the coral. Inside its enormous mouth, we saw along the picket fence of fine sharp teeth a little fish, gaily tidying up the place.

Before surfacing, I came upon a black sea hedgehog, whose poisonous spines are seven or eight inches long, and beside it a big shell to which many legends are attached. The Tridacna lay upon the ocean floor half open, waiting there like a trap, its wavy edges looking graceful but menacing, with their flesh-like lips of bright colour. As I approached, the shell snapped shut with a firmness that showed great strength. This characteristic, I knew, had given rise to most of the legends—of poor pearl divers whose hands had been caught by the Tridacna and who were held fast until they drowned.

34

Later, some of us experimented with the shell's powers. It is true that on the bottom, a hand cannot be freed easily. But you can pull the shell from the sand without much trouble, surface, and pry it open without either much pain or difficulty.

You have probably seen the Tridacna more often than you think, for they are commonly used in churches as shallow fonts for holy water.

I was lying on the sand at Sceik Said, soaking up a little warm sunshine before returning to the depths, and heard Baschieri tell the amazing theories of Cousteau concerning such fine 'coral' sands. Most people think they are created by erosion of the sea, but Cousteau believes the parrot fish is responsible. Using its very hard beak, it consumes enormous quantities of madrepore. After digesting it, the fish leave behind them microscopically mashed particles which eventually make so many fine beaches and sandy bottoms of the sea.

Down we dived again, meeting near the coral precipice a school of arbalests with blue horizontal stripes and very long tails. Then the actors in this gaudy stage-setting changed, and we saw many different kinds of butterfly fish. Some were yellow and flat with thin black lines and large dark marks under their eyes, travelling in pairs. Others had dorsal fins that looked like bunches of feathers, and they circled around the madrepore in fours. These were also yellow but had black and white shading in the middle and two horny eyebrows over the eyes. Still others were silver, with brown noses and black tails—the most elegant fish we had seen, until we came upon the rare type with violent-orange vertical stripes on the yellow snout, and another a lovely reddish brown.

So varied are the fishes in the Red Sea, that people are continually finding new ones and making up names for them. Under one common name go some that are closely related but of many different shapes and colours. We saw pigfish, for instance, of as great diversity as the butterfly fish, but they were all armed with horny beaks, like the parrot fish, to eat the madrepore. It was easy to see where this fish got its name: from its prominent and comical nose. The most common type was deep blue, with a big spot on the side.

The tiny coral fish were just as varied. Every time we came close to the madrepore, hundreds of them darted fearfully away, dashing in and out of the tortuous paths in the coral bank. Once inside a little crevice, they stood still, shaking their tails rhythmically, like a heart beating in fear. Coral fish are always small—never more than an inch and a half to two inches long—but they range in colour from white to black, with shades of green, yellow, red. They think they are so safe inside the madrepore that even when a piece is broken off and taken to the surface, the tiny fish remain inside.

I looked into a small dark grotto in the coral and saw a head with enormous eyes. I shot at it, pulled it out, and at once the fish began to swell up like a balloon, and hard, sharp spikes stuck out on all sides. I had caught a porcupine fish which, when disturbed, suddenly swallows an enormous quantity of water to make it swell up. As the skin stretches, its spines stick out two or three inches, making a formidable defensive weapon. Later I encountered a close relative, the ball fish, which has the same strange capacity for blowing itself up, but few or no spikes.

After catching the porcupine fish a shadow passed over my head. I looked quickly, but the visibility was not good enough for me to see more than a shadow. There was no mistaking it, however—shark! Eager to meet our first shark under water, Giorgio and I went down quite deep, hoping to see in the far dark corners some of these creatures which are always in fear of an improvised and unexpected attack. But though we were disappointed, our many voyages permitted us to photograph numerous strange fish that live beyond the coral barrier.

In the muddiness we came upon another kind of arbalest,

which is a more graceful relative of the skate. This one was black, with a white band on his tail. He was very dignified and seemed to be aloof and disdainful of all the brightly coloured fish around him, like a serious gentleman in a dinner jacket at a fancy dress ball.

Then there were spotted fish and striped graylings, travelling in clouds, with the yellow colour predominating. They moved slowly, skimming over rocks that seemed to be formed from an endless flow of lava. Suddenly we saw the flash of many spindle-shaped sardines, followed by majestic red-brown graylings, whose snouts give them a look of perpetual anger. In mid-water we encountered the scad, easiest of all fish to hit with a gun and the one which, when wounded, attracts sharks more than any other. Perhaps this is because they lose such large quantities of blood, but later we had an idea that it was because they shrieked less when in danger.

On the sand at great depths we found the large skates, clumsy brothers of the arbalests up among the coral peaks. Although they appear to be pitch-black, they really have a good deal of yellow on them, with clear dots and light blue-violet circles. But there is nothing quite so beautiful as the panther rays, sweeping gracefully through the water like some aeroplane of the future, their great fins swooping up and down like the wings of birds and their long tails—five or six times the length of their bodies—streaming out behind.

At Sceik Said we first encountered suicide in the marine world. Gigi Stuart caught one of those big rays known as devil-fish, one of several types with a short stinging sword under the base of the tail. As Gigi brought it to the surface, struggling at the end of the arrow, the ray's sword-tail whipped around in a great contortion and stuck in its own side. A shudder and the fish was dead! At the time we thought this was strange, but just a coincidence, an accident that had happened in the course of the creature's struggles. But a month later Gigi and Gianni

37

caught another devilfish, brought it to the surface and saw the same thing happen. A bit later I brought one to the surface and the event repeated itself. We were finally convinced that the fish, seeing itself lost, chooses death rather than capture.

This was the kind of thing we were busy learning at Sceik Said while we waited for the permits to work where we wanted.

4

Nacuda, Barracuda, and Negus

THE twelve of us climbed into one taxi in Massaua and went south to the little village of Archico. The taxi was an old reliable automobile which had been the gift of Mussolini to a famous Ethiopian *ras*, and its present chauffeur travelled always with several cakes of ice 'to keep from dying of the heat'. That was why, when we opened the doors of the car, streams of water flowed out on our feet.

I found a convenient place on the right running-board, to the envy of all the others who coveted this coolest of spots. We rattled off, leaving behind us a long wet strip from the melting ice, and finally arrived at our destination. When the dusty coast turned green and soft we were in Archico, an African village like most of those along the shore, where we saw first of all an old Turkish fort and wondered what in the world the Turks were doing there. Then we saw huts in indescribable confusion; some outdoor tables at a café at which the only customers were millions of flies; a few camels looking at us both stupidly and menacingly; a thousand little boys every square rod; and Enza Bucher buying a coloured cushion. Enza bought cushions everywhere she went, and some day I am going to Naples to visit her home and see what she has done with them all.

We were photographed in Archico as we had been everywhere else, and obviously we must have been in high spirits, because for the first time the usual arrangement in order of precedence with Vailati in the centre, flanked by Baschieri and Bucher, was not observed.

We came to Archico to look for an Arab *nacuda*, giving Vailati a chance to show off his Arabic. A nacuda is a man who has navigated sampans all over the little known routes of the Red Sea since childhood. He is indispensable to anyone who wants to get off the beaten track in this sea filled with reefs and shoals.

Nacudas are held in great esteem in these regions, and are called 'chief' because they have travelled to many places and met many different people. But they are not necessarily considered decent and honest. Some have made great reputations as pirates. A few have been known to ferry pilgrims on the way to Mecca to an unknown island and leave them there to die after robbing them. They are never found out, for the voyage is undertaken in secret in the first place, nobody knows the islands, and the thousands of crabs will dispose of the remains in no time. It is no wonder that the nacudas are surrounded with a halo of mystery and frightened respect. Honest or dishonest, they are all obviously cunning and intelligent. One of them, called Ato Joseph, told us an amusing story to prove this.

Joseph had become good friends with a Frenchman, and they had sailed together for many years dealing, so it was said, in the slave traffic. They decided to organise a colossal swindle, of the sort that would only have been possible about fifty years ago when this happened. They bought up for almost nothing a great collection of exotic gifts and stolen goods, all duly labelled with the official papers of the state of Abyssinia. Then they journeyed to St. Petersburg, where Ato presented his gifts and fake credentials to the Tsar, whose officials never bothered to check them. For about two years, the two lived royally at the court, until one day they announced that they were returning to their country for a rest. They filled their valises with all the valuable objects they could lay their hands on, and were given precious gifts for the Menelik. It was only much later that the truth came out, and no one was ever able to identify or locate the 'ambassadors'.

I must reassure you at once that the nacuda we found, and had with us for five months, never tried to leave us to the crabs on a desert island or carry us to the Court of St. James's as phony ambassadors. Our nacuda was of the highest intelligence and the greatest ability. But he was not easy to find.

We went first to Shek Sherif, a kind of local witch doctor, followed by a mass of people who yelled, screamed and laughed. The witch doctor, we were told, knew all the nacudas of the Red Sea and could recommend the best.

When we approached, Shek Sherif came out on the road dressed all in red, carrying a red banner, and singing a hymn at the top of his voice. Vailati thereupon showed off his Arabic, as follows:

VAILATI: My friend, tell me, who is the best nacuda round here?

SHEK SHERIF (*singing, skipping twice, and waving his banner*): Allah is great and we must all pray to Allah.

VAILATI (*always serious*): All right, my friend, but tell me . . .

SHEK SHERIF (*still singing, jumping, and waving the banner again*): The roads to Allah cannot be seen. The Prophet tells us to pray to Allah.

Vailati, patiently, but with growing concern, repeated his request.

Shek Sherif, also patient, repeated his statements about Allah, with variations.

After a quarter of an hour, Vailati turned to us with a strange gleam in his eyes, and said, 'Let's give up. The fellow is mad.'

At this point, Shek Sherif grabbed his arm and muttered in broken Italian, 'Come with me. I'll find you a nacuda, but you have to give me two dollars.'

That's how we found a pilot for the *Formica*—Asgodom, a young native who turned out to be cunning, intelligent, and a tireless worker.

41

We now had the pilot but nowhere to go. A week had already passed, and we still did not have our work permits. Vailati pulled every string he knew, and Bucher even made a quick trip to Asmara to hurry things along. But we had to keep on working at Sceik Said.

I was on watch with the scientific group, sitting on the sea floor and wielding a hammer against the base of a madreporic spire that we intended to bring to the surface. Suddenly I had the strange sensation that someone was looking at me over my shoulder. I turned and saw, just about eighteen inches away, the frightening face of a huge barracuda.

It was thin and long, very long—about seven feet. It held its tail high and very still and looked at me with one wide-open eye. Its mouth was slightly open, and I could see distinctly the line of the big triangular teeth that give this fish such a terrible appearance. It reminded me of an alligator. Here was the famous pirate of the tropical seas, the fish that natives fear even more than sharks.

My heart was beating fast, and I glanced toward the surface. I moved brusquely and, with a flip of its tail, the fish moved about a yard away—but no more. I leapt for the surface, opened my mouthpiece, and yelled as loudly as I could, 'Barracuda! A barracuda seven feet long!' Then I went down again.

The worst place to meet a dangerous fish is on the surface of the water. That is the place where he finds dead or wounded creatures, the place where he may remember attacking other animals. I knew this was true the moment I put my head under water again, for the barracuda was coming straight toward me. I swam down as fast as I could, knowing I was safer below but not feeling sure how safe. The bottom was not very far down, only about twenty-five feet, and I stopped with my feet in the sand. The barracuda followed me.

42

Had my friends heard my call? I was not sure, as I had not dared take the time to find out. The barracuda started to circle round me, the way sharks do, each time coming a little nearer to me. I didn't have anything to frighten him with. The hammer was too small.

The madrepore! With a push of my fins I moved over and picked up the big branch I had hammered loose. I brandished it before the fish threateningly. He looked startled and uncertain; and his circles grew wider. He kept his eyes on me, went on swimming round me, but ever farther and farther away. I waved my coral branch occasionally, until he was lost to sight in the cloud of plankton.

Looking up, I saw Cecco and Gianni swimming on the surface, carrying guns. With a quick flip, I went up to them, placing myself in the middle for protection.

'But where is he?' Baschieri asked, a little dubious. This was the first time we had met anything like this, and he thought that in my excitement I had exaggerated a bit.

'Underneath,' I said. 'Let's go down.'

We dived, roamed about for twenty seconds and then—there it was, jumping around. With quick glances, Cecco and Gianni begged my pardon for doubting me. They moved toward the fish with their guns, but it moved out of range and disappeared. We could not find him again.

Surfacing, we talked excitedly. Gigi came by and we told him about it. Now it was his turn to be doubtful.

'Well, maybe it's four or five feet,' he grinned indulgently, then dived. Twenty seconds went by, then he bobbed up again.

'By God!' he yelled. 'I shot it! I shot it!'

He pulled the gun out of the water. It was broken in half. The barracuda had been beneath his feet while he was asking us about it. When he dived he had found it in range and shot it. Then there had been a burning jerk and Gigi had found himself holding the butt of the gun. The barracuda had dis-

43

appeared with the harpoon in his side and pulling behind him the sounding line and barrel.

That evening we all talked about these exciting events, and the others expressed doubt about the size of our fish. But fate helped us. We learned the next day that a fisherman in the city had caught a particularly big barracuda in his net. We hurried to see him, and he told us that he had found the fish floating with his stomach in the air and a harpoon in his body, just a few miles from Sceik Said. It was our barracuda, but the fisherman didn't have him any longer because he had taken him to the plant that makes fish meal.

We hurried off to the gates of the most putrefied building one can imagine, arriving at eleven o'clock at night. The night watchman opened the gate a little fearfully to twelve noisy people, and showed us the beast in the icebox. Even without his head, which had been cut off, he measured almost seven feet. That ended all discussion.

Out next specimen was a guitarfish, related both to sharks and skates. Vailati had been taking a little time off after all his trouble trying to get the work permits. He was down in the water and saw the fish coming toward him. Bruno, whose greatest asset as a sportsman is his speed, surprised him, pointed his gun, and hit him squarely in the middle. The scientific group was particularly pleased with the specimen, which for a time hung proudly astern by its tail.

As the sun was setting that evening we saw a slim white American destroyer on which we learned the Negus was planning to make a trip to Djibouti. We were all on the *Formica*, tied up at the same old pier in Massaua, when a fat red-faced man in white shorts and shirt leaned out of a small car and waved his hands. Scrambling from the car, he ran towards us, shouting, 'The Negus! The Negus!'

We didn't pay much attention, because we had heard that

shout every time the Emperor made his little tour of the port, but this time the man came right up to us. 'The Negus!' he shouted. 'He is coming to visit you, and is on the point of arriving!'

We asked a few questions to make sure the man wasn't lying, then ran below to our cabins to put on something more decent than our bathing suits. We heard in the distance a fanfare of trumpets, signal that the Negus was about to leave the Governor's Palace, where he stays in Massaua. Vailati yelled the news that he had just learned that the Emperor would not actually come aboard the *Formica* but would remain on the pier. Since he apparently was interested in our equipment, we decided that we would have to take it ashore where he could view it.

We had four minutes for this job, while he drove from the palace to the port. We managed to get from the hold, in that time, about a dozen guns, spears, harpoons, respirators, tanks, masks, and fins. I lugged out a huge camera, somebody else big pieces of coral, and others a case of beautiful shells. Finally the guitarfish was tossed to the pier. The Emperor arrived, and Bruno told us that he was going to use this opportunity to speak to him about the permits.

The Emperor was at the port but he had not come to our pier or to our boat. Where was he? We waited for twenty minutes before deciding something had gone wrong. We started putting everything away.

Then someone saw a long cortege of cars driving along the seashore. Quickly we dragged everything out again and put it on display. Finally we saw the big blue Cadillac. It slowed down—but it did not stop. The Negus leaned from the car window and looked at us and at our fine display. He nodded in friendly fashion as he went by. We learned later that he had planned to visit us before going aboard the American destroyer, but had been delayed. The Viceroy came to look us over instead.

Despite our disappointment, I wanted pictures of the Negus

45

as he boarded the destroyer, whose pier was only about three hundred yards away. I grabbed my camera and ran along behind the cars. I wondered how the Ethiopian guards would like my running ahead of the Emperor taking pictures, but I didn't slow down. I heard cannons being fired in his honour.

I caught up with him as he stood at the foot of the ladder. He looked at me with laughing eyes and then went up slowly, knowing I was taking pictures of him. The Negus was followed by an old man who looked like someone out of a De Sica film. He was Ras Cassan, the first Ethiopian *ras* who had submitted to the Italian forces in 1935. After the war, when the Negus had returned to Ethiopia, the Emperor had condemned Ras Cassan to follow behind him for the rest of his life, to assist him, and to be a witness of all the triumphs of the Negus.

Meanwhile, down at the *Formica*, the Viceroy was inspecting our equipment. There was a great deal of confusion, with the Viceroy acting like a baby in a toy shop. He wanted to see everything, and would not leave until Vailati promised to teach him how to fish. Then Bruno took up the matter of the permits. The next day, 6 February, we got them at last.

5

Timid Sharks

It took us little time to load the *Formica* and head for Dissei, in the Gulf of Zula, our first stop in the Dahlak Archipelago. We saw before us a long, twisted, mountainous island, from which sprouted long, withered, umbrella-shaped trees. After anchoring in a little bay, on the shores of which stood the huts of the village, we busied ourselves loading our material into small launches. The first boat set out with Baschieri and the scientific group, heading for a large shoal extending northward. Bucher and his sports companions went off towards a rock which, the nacuda said, was a sort of sharks' club. We left last, with Bruno accompanying us.

At a spot that looked rather clear, Bruno and I jumped into the water, while the boat stayed near by with its motor shut off. Below, we found a huge, dark-red forest—rising up from a depth of about sixty-five feet in thick clumps like giant bushes—which cast deep mysterious shadows. From the top of the jungle rose tufts of seaweed, thin, long, and wavering, from which hung large seeds.

The forest was populated with myriads of fish, some tiny black ones with white spots and, farther away, silvery fish, scads moving in groups. Some of the seaweed stung like nettles when we touched them, but we went on down to the bottom as explorers with a definite aim. Moving ahead with difficulty through the red entanglement, we cut samples of seaweed and other plants, tied them to corks to send them to the surface, where

47

those in the boat would pick them up. This was part of our general plan of studying the vegetation on the sea bottom to discover if man could take advantage of it. Some sea plants might contain important chemicals, pharmaceutical aids, or other valuable elements. Perhaps some could be transplanted and cultivated, enabling a real underwater agriculture to develop.

This is an example of the way in which we wanted to be pioneers of the Blue Continent. We did not intend to colonialise it or become exploiting profiteers. The road was open to all, to specialists in every field. We just wanted to point the way and show that it led somewhere worth while.

While Bruno and I were carrying on our routine work, the two other groups were having some adventures with sharks. Bucher and his companions had plunged into the water near their rock, only to find it so turbid that a whale might have been there without their seeing it. But just as they were about to move, a small shark about five feet long passed near Raimondo, who shot it. It showed its spirit immediately by leaping out of the water and biting away a piece of the small boat.

Less than a mile to the north, Gianni Roghi shot at a young shark while he was in only about seven feet of water. The beast was wounded in a non-vital part, and when it began its 'epileptic' dance, it got the sounding line tangled in a big madrepore. Then it thrashed its tail about wildly and lost a lot of blood. Roghi, not wanting to lose it, grabbed the gun and stood firm, but after a moment the lashing was so violent that he could not hold on any longer. From afar, the others could see him in the midst of a great lathery foam, rising, sinking, then rising again. Finally, while Gigi and Cecco were swimming furiously to his aid, the shark gave a tremendous wrench that actually burst the madrepore, broke the sounding line, and sent it away to die alone.

Noon came, and everyone rested for a few minutes after lunch, then we went back to work again. Ten men and two women moved about under water, taking photographs, hunting, collecting coral, observing the actions of a small crab, trying to get a shark within range of the movie camera. There was our expedition, working happily just as we had imagined and calmly going about a variety of tasks, at depths of sixteen, sixty-five, twenty-five, a hundred, seven, and fifty feet in the water. It was the picture of hundreds of other afternoons and mornings, of people at work in a new world. That fact alone proved to us that our ideas about possible development of the Blue Continent were not Utopian.

The next day I was descending toward the bottom along a steep bank of madrepore. From two enormous umbrella-like pieces of coral, a shark lumbered up slowly toward me. We both kept moving toward each other, cautiously and slowly Perhaps the beast felt encouraged because I carried no harpoon like the others. Perhaps he was attracted by the red fins, which I was wearing instead of my customary black ones. In any event, he kept advancing, and so did I. When we were about six feet apart, my friend began to go away, but with great dignity.

I grabbed hold of a piece of jutting rock so that I might stand still and see what would happen next. He turned back toward me again, diagonally, to keep an eye on me. The eye is perhaps the most awesome part of a shark—greenish yellow, like a cat's phosphorescent eye, with a narrow black line cutting it. No, it was not a pleasant eye he kept on me. The shark was curious, wanted to find out what kind of fish I was. He would have liked to approach closer, but was a little afraid. Now that I was still, he didn't know how to make the next move. Suddenly he hunched up, then stretched out again, like a whip, flashed in a wide circle around me, and disappeared. The situation had been a little awkward for both of us, but he had resolved it neatly. While I surfaced, I mentally went over the *Shark Manual* which Vailati had given me and decided that I had just met a black-tip shark.

As I came out of the water I saw the boat of our distinguished guests, the Italian and British Ministers to Eritrea, who had come to spend a day with us and watch the work. They listened with great anxiety to my story, then observed with interest the complicated manœuvres I had to go through to reload the movie camera. It was easier than usual because there was a wonderfully smooth sea. Sounds from the other boats came to us clearly.

One of the sounds was the clamour and excitement following the capture of a large ray that struggled violently. We saw Bucher diving and emerging, shouting orders, and then pulling the large fish out of the water. It was a perfect flying saucer, such as you can see illustrated in American magazines. Round in shape—flat on the bottom, spherical on top—with two blackish eyeballs in front inside two cavities. It was all yellow, with hundreds of little thorns sticking out from its tough skin.

Bucher had run into it while swimming on the bottom, and his gun had perforated the tough hide because of the great force of its compressed springs. But hitting it was not enough. The ray weighed more than a hundred pounds, and a hundred pounds arranged in that shape is very hard to handle. Some of the others had had to go down and help Raimondo recover it.

After reloading the camera I went down again with Giorgio to film an immense coral reef jutting out from the madreporic bank. I pointed out the spot from which he should take the picture, and he dived down with the camera to place himself in a crevice in the rock. In a moment I followed, and when I was beside the coral, turned to see if he was ready. To my amazement I saw only the camera sitting on the floor of the sea and no Giorgio. Then I saw him heading for the surface like a rocket. I went up, too, to see what had happened.

'A moray, an enormous moray!' he shouted. 'I had my face right close to it.'

'Where?'

'Right in my crevice in the rock, where I wanted to take pictures,' he complained.

While he swam to the boat to get the gun, I went down to

see for myself. There it was—a huge one. Its head, rocking a bit, with the mouth opening and closing, stared out at me with a superior and unfriendly expression. I could understand the shock it must have given Giorgio when he started to swim into the crevice.

Giorgio returned with the gun. The shot had to be exact and precise, for the moray could cause us plenty of trouble if wounded only superficially. Fortunately the shot was perfect, and the spear went in right behind the moray's head. It drew back inside the hole at once, so Giorgio abandoned the gun and grabbed the end of the disappearing spear. He pulled and tugged, but got nowhere. Then he braced his legs against the rock and pulled harder. It was incredible. I saw Giorgio actually being pulled into the crevice, so I dropped the camera with which I was filming the marvellous scene and ran to help him. Together we pulled with all our might, gained an inch or two, and felt that we were winning. Then with a sudden snap, the harpoon attached to the spear, although it was made of a special armour-plated steel, was broken in two.

Giorgio and I rose to the surface panting, scrambled into our small boat and lay down to rest. In five or ten minutes we heard Zecca yelling from his boat some distance away, 'Come! Come! I've caught an enormous moray! Hurry up!'

We rowed toward him as fast as we could, noticing that the water round his boat was splashing as if the boat were being rocked. Inside was a tremendous moray weighing twenty-nine pounds. It had been beautifully hit by a well-placed harpoon.

Of course we told Zecca that we had just seen one like that, but it had got away—the old fish story. Then when he had finished the kill by piercing the beast's head, we found our harpoon in its neck.

'My God, where did this come from?' Zecca asked.

'From here,' Giorgio said, showing him the point of our spear, from which the harpoon had broken off.

51

We rushed to photograph the beautiful specimen which had been caught, more or less, by all three of us. Later we learned a much less fatiguing way of handling the moray. After it is hit, it retires into its hole, bleeds, and tires itself out. Then you can go back and pull it out easily.

On 9 February we left Dissei *en route* for the largest island of the Dahlak Archipelago. Great Dahlak is half as large as Corsica and of volcanic origin. We entered a large channel whose sides were formed by enormous black and red masses eaten away by the sea and falling straight into the water. Some day, when men reach Mars and travel through the crevices of that planet, they will see something like that.

In the evening we roamed through the town in our jeep and were greeted by the usual Arab hospitality—a hospitality that was rather hard to take, since every time we stopped we were invited to eat at least one raw egg and drink two or three cups of coffee and as much tea. We could manage the egg, but the so-called aromatic coffee had an aroma that we didn't like— reminding us of roast meat. By midnight we had reached the point when another cup of coffee or tea would have made us sick, and Masino told us, trembling slightly, that we were about to be served tepid camel's milk. Fortunately, it did not arrive.

All of the people we talked to wanted to discuss sharks. One young fellow told us about a big shark that lived in the wreck of a ship. In the hold there were cases and cases of silver coins, and pearl fishers would dive down at night—to elude the guard posted above the boat—to try to find some of the treasure. But the shark ate them all, one by one, until it grew bigger and bigger. After two years, when it was truly a monster, the shark ate a handsome young man whose father determined to avenge the death of his son. He got in his boat and baited a huge steel hook with half a goat. The shark bit immediately and a violent struggle began. The water foamed, and became redder and redder. Even after hours of battling, the old man in the boat held on, and finally at dawn the shark gave up, and its white belly could be seen on the surface. The whole town had come to the shore to see the old man bring in the beast, and it measured more than twenty-three feet in length.

We must have looked rather sceptical at this tale, for the young man said, 'Wait and see,' and then left.

While we waited for him to return, we heard another score of stories about sharks—ferocious, aggressive, fearful sharks. First, a story about a fisherman who had been killed; next, one about a man with a leg chewed off; and so on.

The young man came back holding a big jaw of whitish bone.

'Here is the head,' he said, putting it on the floor.

We looked at it carefully, saw the six rows of slightly curved and jagged teeth, the biggest more than an inch long.

'Now, do you believe me?' the young native asked triumphantly.

Yes, we believed him—at least about the size of the shark. Baschieri said that from the size of the jaw he would estimate that the creature must have weighed five or six hundred pounds and run about twenty-three feet in length. It had been a tiger shark, one of the most feared of all sharks.

The tiger shark is quite different from other sharks in that it has excellent eyesight, while the others see poorly. It swims along on the surface of the water, with its eyes above the waves, and can spot a fisherman's boat three miles away. Then he starts for the boat, swimming faster and faster, until he cracks into it at high speed and the fisherman is out of the boat and into the shark's mouth before he knows what has happened.

We talked about life on the island, and Zecca mentioned the cows he had seen roaming about the huts like gaunt spectres. Some of the natives spoke of the scarcity of vegetation, and one man told us how he collected the seaweed washed ashore by the waves. He dried it and fed it to his cattle. We all looked at each other and smiled at this verification of our belief that men could use the plants from the floor of the sea much more than they do. Places like Dahlak could become richer and provide good diets for their people and animals if men would only learn how to use the wealth around them in the water instead of waiting for the waves to wash it in to them in tiny quantities.

The next morning something was wrong with my stomach. It might have been the things I had drunk in the village or the beer I had had with my milk for breakfast, but my head began to spin as we were on our way to the island of Nokra. I had to return to the *Formica* and give up work for the day, which made me miss an epic adventure.

When Bruno, Giorgio, and Masino came back to the *Formica*, I saw the shark Bruno had captured, and my fever went up in my anger at having missed it. This was what had happened.

While Masino was in the small boat and Giorgio was ashore taking some pictures, Bruno went into the water. He came across a large dentex and shot it, but the fish lost a lot of blood in the struggle. Within a few seconds a shark appeared, about seven feet long. It tried to grab the wounded dentex, but Bruno yelled at him so loudly that he let go. Giorgio heard what was going on and entered the water, and by that time more sharks appeared until the sea seemed filled with them. They were all good-sized sharks, from seven to ten feet long—about twenty of them. Giorgio, the only one who had never seen a shark, got a real baptism. The two men descended together, Bruno handling his gun and Giorgio taking pictures. The speedy sharks zigzagged, criss-crossed, and circled around them.

'I'll never forget that scene as long as I live,' exclaimed Giorgio.

Masino laughed, and told how he watched the sharks' fins all over the water while the other two were below. They were down quite a while, for it was several minutes before Bruno

The legendary Tridacna, largest shell in the world, which supposedly traps and kills unwary pearl fishers. Although it snaps shut at the approach of danger and may hold a man's hand tightly, it can be opened.

Taking submarine movies with our large camera, whose watertight case is equipped with horizontal and vertical stablizers for balance and mobility.

In the total darkness of a cave at a depth of 160 feet,
our flash bulb revealed some of the most brilliant colors
of the Blue Continent.

A school of butterfly fish moves elegantly
over the floor of the Red Sea.

Polychrome tufts of Alcyonaria, submarine
plantlike animals that float in great numbers
through tropical oceans.

The underwater photographer catches a shot of the tiny coral-fishes that hide in the labyrinths of Madre-poral clumps.

A few samples of the infinite variety of exotic fish in
the Red Sea, with a parrot fish at the upper left.

A blue crab with nippers measuring twelve to fourteen inches, which our cameras nearly missed because its color almost matched the surrounding Madrepore.

shot his harpoon. It was the first time an underwater man had shot at a shark and captured it!

Well, perhaps not exactly the first. The expedition had met sharks before, or members of the shark family. Vailati had caught the guitarfish and Bucher a small shark. Other expeditions had hit small sharks with underwater guns. But this was really a first kill in the true sense because Bruno's was a big shark, measuring about ten feet. It belonged to the man-eating species. It was captured in the midst of other sharks by only one diver under very precarious conditions—muddy water, slight depth, and strong current.

Bruno explained carefully just what had happened. A shark had come toward him, then turned to flee. At that moment, Bruno wheeled round and fired, hitting the beast squarely. This was the dramatic moment. How would that shark react? What would his friends do?

Bruno expected the shark to come back at him furiously. The water was red with blood so Bruno could not see clearly. But the shark tried to run away. When he realised this, Bruno grabbed Giorgio by the hand so that he could stand the expected force of the shark's pull. But there was no need. The shot had been perfect, striking near the liver, so the creature was lifeless within a few seconds.

This raised a further problem. If they tried to take the dead shark to the surface, would the other sharks attack it and try to devour it, as they were said to do? Or would they attack the man who had had the audacity to kill one of them?

They did neither. Bruno and Giorgio took the shark to the surface while the other sharks just went on circling about, until they finally left the area as if frightened by what had happened.

Bruno's exploit taught us a tentative lesson about sharks that we had not known before, something of importance to the safety of amphibious man working in the Blue Continent. There is no danger of attack from a shark for the submerged man—even

55

when the shark is large and dangerous, even if he is in the midst of many other sharks, even if he is attacked and hit. It was a great victory, but we all looked forward to more experiences that would verify our conclusions.

The next day I was still a little weak from my sickness, but I was determined not to miss any new adventure. I asked the chief, Bruno, if I might go out with them on the boats, promising I would not dive. He said something which, by stretching a point, I could take to mean yes, so I joined a small boat heading for the channel between Great Dahlak and Nocra. Another passenger was thin and scrawny Idris, one of three native fishermen we had recruited. A man of about thirty, he always had a very sad expression on his face, and a nose that never seemed to end. On his wrist he wore a bracelet with many small silver and leather boxes which, he said, contained prayers for good luck, health, love, and success in war. The prayers began to function whenever he moved his arms, thus saving him the time and effort of stopping to pray five times a day.

My friends dived and I had to sit in the boat under a ridiculous sun helmet. But the silence was broken in a few moments by Bruno, who appeared near the boat.

'A hundred-pound cernia!' he yelled, and disappeared.

I sat up with a start. I was familiar with cernias, of course, but in the Mediterranean a fifty or sixty-pound cernia is considered a catch that one can talk about for the rest of the season. Here was something out of the ordinary.

Why is the cernia thought a considerable prize by the underwater hunter? This close relative of the West Indian grouper is neither the rarest, largest, nor best fish one can catch in the sea. But it is one of the cleverest antagonists, a courageous and stubborn beast. It does not flee before man but goes to meet him, then keeps itself just out of range with a flip of its tail. In retreat, it always turns and looks the enemy in the face.

The cernia is not a transitory fish, but stays in his well-chosen home, a secure cave or grotto with emergency exits. Year after year, fishermen find the same cernia in the same place, and some have become legendary, outwitting all the skilled hunters who have tried to catch them.

When hit in his cave, the cernia puts up a tremendous fight, edging itself into the rock, swelling itself up with water so that it fits tightly against the walls, striking tremendous blows with its thorny fin or large tail. Sometimes the battle is only won when the hunter succeeds in planting his fingers in the cernia's eyes, which paralyses it and allows it to be brought to the surface. Bruno told a story about one particularly stubborn cernia. It stuck in its cave so fast that the line from the arrow was finally attached to a motorboat which started pulling. The cable stretched, the boat tugged, but the cernia did not give up—not until the head snapped off. That was all the hunter got, for the body remained in the cave.

And now Bruno had found a cernia of a hundred pounds! If it lived up to the reputation of its species, there should be a tremendous battle. It had started already, for Bruno surfaced, crying, 'I've got it, but give me another harpoon so I can shoot it again.'

I handed it to him, and he dived. I looked round to see if there was anyone who could help, but Zecca and Bucher, who were the nearest, were about six hundred yards away. It was useless to call them.

Bruno appeared again. 'Is there another gun?' he demanded. I handed him mine, the only one left in the boat, and down he went. I muttered under my breath. Did I have to miss this wonderful spectacle just because of a stupid stomach?

It took me only a second to put on my gear, forget the doctor's orders, and dive into the water wishing I had my camera with me. About twenty-five feet down the water was very clear and there, next to a mass of coral, I saw a cernia as long as Vailati. A kind of underwater elephant, it had instead of tusks the two

57

harpoons Bruno had shot into it. But they apparently had no more effect than toothpicks. When Bruno started to shoot a third time, the beast seemed to comprehend that this strange man could be a nuisance with those arrows, so with a flip of its tail it went out of range. Then two more swishes of the tail, and it disappeared.

Bruno returned to the surface as mad as a hatter, and we spent ten minutes in the boat, swearing, until we heard yelling from Bucher and Zecca. By the time we got there, we saw a huge cernia being lifted into Bucher's boat—the cernia that had escaped Bruno's gun only to take refuge in the worst possible spot in the whole archipelago, the place where Bucher and his men were fishing.

Zecca had seen it first and could not make out what kind of fish it was, with its two strange horns. Diving closer, he nearly had heart failure to see such an immense cernia with two harpoons stuck in it. Bucher came to his aid, but momentarily they lost the beast in the muddy water. Then Zecca saw it again in the shadow of a reef and remained on top of the reef to cut off its escape while Bucher went down to shoot it. He hit it squarely, grabbed the spear, and found himself with the broken shaft in his hands. Since the fish did not appear to be much bothered by the three shots it had received, Bucher stuck two fingers in its eyes and tried to put his arms round it to pull it to the surface. But the cernia gave such a violent swish of its tail that Raimondo rolled away under water like a ball, half knocked out and badly scratched.

He did not give up, however. The hunter returned to the boat and loaded his gun with a secret weapon, his own invention, embodying in one piece the harpoon and the spear. Down he went again, and found the cernia right away, in another crack of the rock. Raimondo pointed his gun and shot. The spear went in deep, and another followed it immediately, from Zecca's gun. He knew that his weak gun could never have penetrated the thick skin and skull of the beast—we learned later that the bone of the skull was an inch thick—so he aimed for the same hole made by Bucher's harpoon and hit the mark.

Next, the fight began to drag the fish to the surface. Five shots by three men had not put it out of action, so Bucher grabbed hold of it with a strong sounding line. The giant cernia made violent convulsions and turned toward the high seas to look for another cave. But Bucher grabbed one of the spears and held on. While he was being pulled through the water at high speed, he managed to wrap the line tightly round the fish's neck and gills. With Zecca helping, he finally managed to bring the cernia to the surface and, after a short struggle, get it into the boat.

Things were never dull. The next day I was in the water surrounded by blackfin sharks seven and eight feet long. Ten of them insisted on staying together down near the bottom on the other side of a small madreporic barrier in front of the island of Nokra. I tried my best to get near them, but they fled like streaks of lightning out to sea. So I borrowed a gun, shot a fish, and threw it into the water half dead. When the sharks began to take an interest in it, I dived as slowly as possible and then crawled along the sand to hide behind some gobletlike sponges a foot and a half high.

Finally I came close to a group of three sharks; I stood almost still, turned on my back, put my eye to the view finder, and started taking pictures. They heard the whirring sound, jumped, saw me, and acted as though scared to death. They disappeared again, followed by all the others near by. Time after time I tried to get near enough for good pictures, but they were too frightened. I surfaced for a while, hoping they would take courage and come back.

I prayed for a shark about six feet from my nose, and for once my prayer was granted. The sharks came back, and I did a complicated manœuvre to approach them, changing my strategy. Instead of diving near the coast and swimming out, I swam out first and then dived, so as to block their retreat to the high sea. I hoped that if they suddenly found themselves between me and the coast, they would be befuddled for a few seconds, and I should have time for some pictures.

I advanced along the bottom, getting nearer and nearer. Then I started the movie camera. At the buzzing sound, the nearest sharks saw me, and there was a little commotion in the group—exactly what I wanted. I went on shooting and advancing, and they started fleeing on both sides. One passed right over me. I kept on going, because there was still one left, with his back towards me.

When he finally saw me, I was very close to him. It was probably somewhat dangerous because the shark was terribly frightened, feeling itself trapped between a man and a rock. For one moment he remained still, turning his head from right to left, and wagging his tail. Suddenly, he made three brief but violent strikes toward me, each time coming to about a foot and a half in front of my face. By this time, no doubt, both of us were half dead from fright. I stopped shooting and let myself sink down to the bottom, as if to tell him he could go away if he wanted. He darted away, and the adventure ended.

It's true that I forced the issue, but I was able to say that I had been 'attacked' by a shark.

The following day was even more exciting, for Bucher repeated Bruno's exploit of capturing a shark in a similar way—but this one was even larger. And this time I was in the water, able to see the whole thing.

Since it was larger, or perhaps because it was not hit in such a vital spot, Bucher's shark immediately started pulling with great force, racing toward the open sea. Raimondo, Grazioli, and I grabbed hold of the sounding line and found ourselves racing through the water about sixty feet below the surface. Then the beast gave up and we were able to get it into the boat.

Like Bruno's, it lay there wriggling slightly, opening and closing its round mouth and its yellowish eyes that no longer frightened us. We wished that some of the natives with their shark legends and terrible fear could see them. The Kings of the Sea had been met and equalled in their own elements by underwater men, and there was nothing terrifying about them to us.

The day ended with Giorgio's capture of a big moray. The small boat was there when Giorgio surfaced and threw the moray, huge and squirming, into it. There was a thud and a scream, and Idris leaped into the water, although he didn't know how to swim. We fished him out, while Giorgio held his sides with laughter. Idris did not laugh at all, and made us all promise that we would never play tricks on him again.

The next day we moved to a new spot.

6

Trumpets, Keys, Balls and more Sharks

DURING the prehistoric volcanic explosion that brought the Dahlak islands to the surface of the Red Sea, a piece of molten magma landed on the far side of Entedebir Island and cooled off. Although Cundabilu showed only a red-brown, barren cliff, the waters around it contained a beautiful madreporic garden in which thousands of fish lived and reproduced under ideal conditions. In time the original block of lava was completely covered by new, large, growing deposits of coral, surrounded by hundreds of peaks and valleys.

When Giorgio and I first dived into the water with our cameras, we were surrounded by a dense cloud of big grey fish with high tails, belonging to the arbalest-skate family. They were so certain that we had no bad intentions that they gathered round us curiously, some of them coming so close—less than ten inches from our lenses—that we could not get them in focus.

Suddenly these 'extras' disappeared and the main actors arrived —sharks shooting along the bottom at great speed, circling and passing close by our sides, but keeping a good distance in front. These, too, were so afraid of submerged men that we had difficulty in getting a good picture of them.

Our hunters appeared, and the sharks became even more cautious. The only time they came closer was right after the firing of a gun, when it was being reloaded. By the time the gun was ready, there was not a sign of them. This gave Bucher an idea, so he came down with two guns—a small one which he shot at a fish, a big one ready for the shark. But they were too jittery and continued to keep out of range.

Suddenly a huge cernia appeared, as big as the one caught by Vailati, Bucher, and Zecca. It swam up right behind Gigi Stuart, who at the moment was busy trying to extract from its cave a fifty-pound cernia that he had just shot. Gigi turned round to look straight into the unpleasant face of this giant monster. It was in range, but Gigi had fired his only harpoon at the smaller cernia. He surfaced quickly, keeping his eyes on the beast, and called Gianni, who had his gun ready.

Roghi dived, but just as he reached the big cernia, it leapt into a cave. Gianni approached it, looking at the beast that poked its face from the hole. Gianni did not know what to do, for a shot that would hit the cernia's head would just bounce off that thick skull without making a scratch. He decided to wait until the fish turned on its side and he could get a shot at the gills. But the cernia seemed to guess Gianni's intention. Suddenly he shot out of the cave with a terrific lunge. Roghi tried to swerve aside, but the fish hit him a glancing blow that sent sent him tumbling along the bottom for several yards.

At that moment Bucher arrived on the scene, saw the huge cernia dart from a valley in the rocks, with Roghi staggering out behind it, dazed and badly scratched. Raimondo followed the cernia down into the depths, the fish travelling at just sufficient speed to keep about one yard beyond range of the gun. Finally Bucher lost it and came to the surface. Knowing the way cernia keep always to one particular cave, the sports group came back again and again to find the giant, but they never saw him.

Late one afternoon, our three small boats were returning from Cundabilu to Dahlak where the *Formica* was anchored. Cecco's boat had a long sounding line let out behind, with a big hook and bait in anticipation of anything interesting that might come along and take a bite.

Huge clouds had darkened the sky, and a strong wind whipped the water into high waves that slowed us down. We shipped water regularly, until we were all soaked, along with our equipment, and bailing furiously to keep afloat. Then the rain came pouring down on us, and at that moment we saw that Cecco's boat had stopped and was turning round. Since we could not hear his shouts in the high wind, those of us in the other two boats turned about and went back to his side. There we found that the sounding line had been caught on a reef and saw Cecco dive into the water.

We turned off our two outboard motors and covered them to keep them dry and waited, drenched and still bailing. In a few seconds Cecco's head appeared and we heard him yell, 'It's a shark!' A shark was caught on the hook and the line was caught on a big coral formation. The boat would have to make a big circle to disentangle the line before anything could be done about the shark. Luckily, all motors started and we began our manœuvre. We knew the line was free when we saw the violent jerks of the shark on it.

Just how Cecco and Gigi managed to get the shark on their boat without capsizing it or going overboard themselves I will never know, but finally it was there, flapping and struggling. Gianni ran up and started hitting it on the head with a big stick, but the shark continued to wrench its tail violently. Cecco tried to catch the tail and tie it down, but could not quite manage it.

The boat disappeared from our view behind a big wave for a moment, but then we heard a shout that the shark was finally conquered. The men hung it up from crossed oars. At that moment it began wriggling again, and opening and closing its mouth. This was the time, with its head up and mouth open, to test the old theory that fresh water would instantly kill a shark if poured in its mouth.

But there was no fresh water on any of the boats! It had been hot in the morning, and we had all finished our bottles. We felt a little silly, drenched to the skin, in the pouring rain, tossed about by high waves, and wondering how we could get some water. But we would go through anything to make a test.

Priscilla Hastings, who had been busy sketching, appeared from under a huge canvas covering. 'I have some tea,' she said in her calm British way, holding out a flask.

Cecco looked at us questioningly, and when none of us said anything he blurted out, 'All right. Let's try it.'

He opened the flask and poured the contents right down the gullet of the shark, which shuddered violently, like some maniac having a fit, and collapsed—thoroughly dead.

Having killed a shark with tea in the middle of a raging storm, we returned to our base with quite a story.

That evening, in discussing sharks, Gigi Stuart said that we ought not to feel too sure about our judgment of them. Up to that time we had not encountered any of the worst anthropophagous varieties, the toughest man-eaters, so he suggested that we should all be wary and draw no final conclusions until we had met some of the dark sharks, or blue sharks, or the even more dangerous tiger sharks. The very next day Giorgio and I met the first dark shark.

All of us went to a bay where we wanted to make some tests on underwater flash pictures. There were clouds of plankton in the shallow water, so we had to swim out beyond them to the open sea, where we never felt quite so much at ease, at least near the surface. The tests were complicated and important, having to do with the possible relation of transparency to the amount of salt in the water. We kept busy for more than an hour, when suddenly I felt apprehensive and turned to see a shark advancing toward us, about a yard below the surface. I poked Giorgio and we both dived.

Without seeing us, the shark passed overhead, and we could

easily distinguish its type. It was quite dark, about eleven feet long, and a man-eater. I glanced at Giorgio and saw that he was calmly loading the camera. Before going on, we planned our strategy in case the shark should return: we would dive about half-way between the surface and the bottom. The only trouble was that we did not have our auto-respirators and could not stay down very long.

The outline of the shark appeared about fifteen feet away. We filled our lungs to the bursting point and dived. The weight of our cameras kept us at just about the point we wanted, and the shark moved slowly toward us—more slowly than any shark I had ever seen. He was probably attracted to us because we were so still that he thought we were corpses, but he couldn't be quite sure. He began to circle, then headed straight for us at great speed. I raised the camera and Giorgio set off the flash. I'm sure I took my picture with my eyes closed. The shark swooshed past us, rocking us a bit, and disappeared. That was a *tête-à-tête* we shall both remember as long as we live, but we had pictures that made all our testing and fright worth while.

The scientific group wanted to gather specimens of coral fish. The best way to make a big haul of these little creatures is to explode a small quantity of dynamite that kills them—and at the same time many bigger and tastier fish, which in turn attract many sharks. Bruno went along as armed escort, and I followed in the hope of getting some good pictures.

We selected a spot with plenty of madreporic growth and set off the dynamite beneath the water. A huge column of foam rose, and we threw ourselves into the water, which was muddy from debris and cluttered with dead fish. In a few seconds the sharks began arriving from all directions. With such poor visibility in the water, we did not feel too comfortable. But they passed us by, grabbed the bigger fish, disappeared, then came back for more. We knew that they would be gone in ten minutes, having eaten everything worth while, but we could not wait that long. The current would carry away the coral fish that our scientists wanted to collect.

So there was an unusual sight—three men swimming all around with small yellow butterfly nets, catching little fish no larger than nails. Swimming with them in the same waters, many hungry sharks, also looking for fish—but larger ones. And on the surface of the water, thousands of dead fish with white bellies showing. Men and sharks worked together side by side, almost ignoring each other. We studied the shark's method of catching a fish by passing over it and opening the mouth to take it in. If the fish was on the surface, the shark stuck his head out of the water enough to get the fish without turning over.

Vailati tried another experiment with the sharks. He shot a scad—considered a choice morsel by sharks—left it on the end of the harpoon, and moved away to see if the sharks would follow. We had always heard that sharks were very cunning and possessed quick reflexes. What we witnessed then, however, caused us to have grave doubts on this point—at least so far as the white-fin variety was concerned. They were the subjects on whom Bruno tried his experiment.

He sat down on a reef and held his gun like a fishing pole, from which extended the sounding line, the spear, the harpoon, and the scad—waving about in midwater. The sharks circled round the dead fish; then one of them decided to take a bite. As it sped toward the scad on a straight line, Bruno moved his bait slightly, but the shark did not alter his direction. It kept going on its set path, closed its mouth on nothing, and started circling again. Another shark made a pass at the fish. Once more Bruno shifted its position slightly, with the same result. For more than ten minutes, Vailati teased the sharks, which were completely puzzled.

Not once did a shark alter its direction to compensate for the movement Bruno gave to the scad, even when he shifted it only a foot or two. No matter how many times they struck at the fish, they could not understand that it would not hold still for them. The dark shark Giorgio and I had met the day before had not appeared very bright, but it had not been as stupid as this.

When Cecco finally shouted to us that the scientists had finished their task, Bruno stopped playing and held the scad still. The biggest shark of the group captured the fish from the harpoon and went away happily, but occupying a new low in our estimation.

We took a day off when the *Formica* returned from Massaua, where it had gone for supplies and mail. It felt good to lie on the beach in the sun for a few hours to rest and dry up the wounds that covered most of us. These were not wounds from sharks, about which the natives and our friends back home in Italy worried so much, but from much smaller things without the wide reputations which inspire terror. Cuts, scratches, and burns— these were the only real physical discomforts we felt, but sometimes they caused plenty of agony. It is difficult to touch madrepore or coral, move your legs among the seaweed, or slide down some underwater rock without getting a cut or scratch of some kind. The burns from fire coral and jellyfish are dreadfully painful. Nor did our wounds heal quickly, because we were immersed so much in extremely salty water. But we forgot them the next day when we went diving again, exploring the Blue Continent.

Giorgio was down with his air respirator, gliding along the bottom with his Rolleiflex looking for subjects to photograph. He had been down quite a while, and the compressed-air tanks were almost empty, when he encountered an enormous cernia —one of the hundred-pound giants. While Giorgio was debating whether he had enough air left to approach the big fish for

68

some pictures, the cernia settled the question by coming toward him. Giorgio stood still, his camera ready, noting the ten little pilot fish hovering about the monster like fighter planes escorting a bomber. Giorgio snapped a picture of the huge head, the glassy eyes, and the ugly mouth with a pilot fish on it; at that moment the cernia decisively put on speed, heading straight for him.

Giorgio decided that he'd better make a run for the surface. The cernia raised its head and looked after him a moment, then decided to follow. Luckily, Giorgio did not get panicky. He turned and with greatly exaggerated movements made for the fish. The cernia stopped, a little intimidated, and when Giorgio was almost on top of it, the fish turned and went away slowly.

'I must frighten it thoroughly,' Giorgio thought. 'Then I can surface in peace.'

But his air tank was empty! He took the last small breath of air and sped towards the surface, trying to keep one eye on the cernia. Coming all the way from a depth of a hundred feet—he was almost asphyxiated by the time his head reached the air —he found himself in a swift current of the Nokra channel that bore him away from the boats at high speed. He yelled, Masino and I jumped in to swim to him, and Idris for once rowed the boat with all his strength. Tired from his long immersion, weighted down by the empty respirators, and wondering when a giant cernia might come at him from below, Giorgio was relieved to be pulled into the boat. But he could hardly wait to get down under once more the next morning, when we both got some wonderful movie shots of unusual fish we had never seen before.

Try to imagine a flounder shaped like a rhombus, with a vertical mouth just behind one front corner, big black vivacious eyes at the top corner, a canary-yellow tail sticking out from the rear of the blue-striped red body.

That is the key fish, one of the many varieties of pigfish. Apart from its curious shape, it has many other unusual characteristics. Every time it sees something it doesn't like, it darts into its hole in the rocks—a hole hardly any bigger than the fish itself. It is so small, in fact, that the key fish cannot turn round in it, so must shift into reverse and back out—a ridiculous-looking procedure. Actually, it is not ridiculous at all. There is a reason for everything in nature, including the movements of the key fish.

This creature's defensive weapon is a long spine shaped like a nail, on its back. Inside his hole, the fish raises the spine against the rock above him, making it impossible to pull it out. You can get it only by pressing the muscle on the back that controls the spine, then turning the fish as you would a key in a lock, and extracting it. That is where the fish gets its name.

We also took pictures of the trumpet fish, which some people call the needlefish. It is as slim as a pencil, yellow, and about eighteen inches long, with a flaring mouth that makes it look as if it should be a member of Louis Armstrong's band.

Then there was a hunchbacked creature that we baptised the rhinoceros fish. It is really a large member of the parrot fish family, weighing seventy-five to eighty-five pounds, and possessing the hard, curved beak of its cousins. I first saw these fish under the reef about fifty feet from the bottom, marching in a line with the largest in front. At my first movement toward them, they were very frightened, and I could not get near them. But I noticed that when they fled, they did so in perfect formation, as if drilled by a strict sergeant-major.

Cousteau, in his report on the Red Sea, said that he had seen rhinoceros fish from afar but had never managed to approach close enough to photograph them. He put forward a theory about the prominent horny hump above their eyes: that they used it to knock off and grind chunks of madrepora, of which all parrot fish eat great quantities. We were later able to test this theory when Bucher managed the great feat of capturing a few rhinoceros

Sixty feet down a magnesium flash lamp surprises a group of small tuna fish.

A diver exploring the wreck meets a myriad of small fish.

Below: a shoal of barracudas photographed ninety feet down. Fortunately the flash lamp frightened them away, as they are armed with a formidable set of teeth (right).

Above: Luigi Stuart Tovin with a captured sea eel.

Some sharks are strangely marked on their heads and bodies.

Left: Silverio Zecca with a large turtle he has caught with his hands. Below: A 450 lb. turtle is hauled aboard while Enza and Raimondo Bucher and Silverio Zecca look on.

Bruno Vailati holding a turtle.

Many-coloured fish weave a fantastic pattern of light and shade before the bewildered gaze of the underwater fisherman.

fish, and we learned that the horn is not hard enough for such work, being actually almost soft. And I was lucky enough to get some fine pictures of them.

We always knew when we were near a school of rhinoceros fish, for we could hear a sound like that of a steam roller passing over a big bag of nuts: the sound of these fish eating. Once I was on the bottom with my camera when a school of twenty rhinoceros fish advanced above me, and I saw that not only did they move in perfect formation but were kept in line by 'officers' which ranged up and down the column, hurrying up the laggards, pushing any rugged individualists back into line.

When I moved, the group experienced a collective panic, the water was broken by the simultaneous flipping of twenty big tails, and the column darted off obliquely on the double. Then they calmed down and moved up to a huge bank of madrepora for their meal. I heard the crackling roar of their grinding beaks as they broke off the rock and chewed it. In twenty minutes they eliminated some of the collected waste matter from their intestines—and white clouds of fine coral sand floated down through the water. This was a possible argument in favour of the hypothesis that rhinoceros fish and their smaller cousins, the parrot fish, create the fine sandy beaches and sea bottoms of a coralline nature.

I did not think I would have much trouble photographing a pair of beautiful ball fish that came along one day, because they looked as if they could be awkward and slow in their movements. But when I dived close and had the view finder to my eye about five feet away, the fish suddenly zigzagged away at high speed. I saw that when they moved their shape changed from round to oval, becoming streamlined according to need. If I had cornered them, they would have swelled up like balloons. They proved what we have always said: that the only accurate way to study fish is to watch them in their natural habitat. If you had this ball fish in a laboratory, how could you tell what

F

shape it was, or how it changed its shape under different circum-stances?

We were diving near the island of Enteara, in the Dahlak group—an island whose sand is so glaringly white that it looks like snow—when we met our first tiger shark, one of the most renowned and feared of all sharks.

The madreporic banks of Enteara drop very suddenly and deeply. Near the surface and for about fifteen feet down, the water was very muddy, but below that it was clear and cool. Diving down through the whitish cloud and finding ourselves suspended on the steep coral wall gave us a tremendous sensa-tion. The wall was brightly coloured and rich with many kinds of fish seen through the diffused light filtering down from above.

I was trying to take a movie of a fisherman immersed in the endless yellow shadows. Bruno, Bucher, and I had somehow moved some distance away from the others when we saw the tiger. It shot out swiftly from the greatest depths but when it saw Bucher, slowed down, turned almost on its side and stared at the human invader. We saw right away that it was not like the sharks we had been encountering. It had a squashed snout instead of the usual streamlined nose, and a very large mouth. Very dark, with big spots, its tail was slim, long, and arched. The description fitted that of the tiger shark, all right, but the spots indicated that ours was a young specimen, for in adults the spots fade away. The size told us it was a youngster, too, for some tiger sharks grow as long as twenty-eight or thirty feet, whereas ours was only fifteen feet. It was big enough, however, to make me have a sudden longing for Rome. It could have made a quick meal of me if it had wanted to.

Bucher and Bruno approached the shark to see how it would behave, and I followed along behind hoping to get a good picture. The shark turned at once and disappeared, just like most of the others we had seen. Perhaps he did flee with greater dignity than the others—but that was all.

Three days later we had a much lengthier encounter with a blue shark, a known man-eater, the protagonist of most of the shark tales of the world and number-one enemy of whalers. In the Red Sea, the blue shark runs smaller than those in the big oceans but somewhat larger than those of the Mediterranean, where they are called *verdone* because of their greenish colour. Everywhere else they are slate grey or steel blue. Ours was metallic blue against the azure blue of the sea, had a long snout and two lateral fins—all of which told us what we were up against.

The hour before the meeting had been spent in the usual way—the scientists collecting their material, our group filming them, Bucher and companions fishing. I found myself with Giorgio near Bruno, who shot a beautiful scad, a favourite dish of the sharks. After hitting it, he let it dangle on the bottom. We waited for several seconds in the large arc formed by the coral barrier, spectators in the seats of an underwater theatre looking out at the stage where the actors would soon appear. Then we saw a black fin, and another, and another. Giorgio emerged from his shelter and flew toward the top. The sharks disappeared. Bruno was on the surface with the gun he had just reloaded.

Then came the blue shark, a majestic sight, fully fifteen feet long—a fine fat fully grown specimen. It advanced with a boldness which was quite different from the attitude of any other shark we had seen, even the tiger. With a flash it came between Giorgio and me, then slowed down and started toward Giorgio, who at that moment was looking through his view finder in another direction, toward a group of six black fins crisscrossing about. He had not seen the blue shark at all.

I stopped filming and dived toward the shark, but since I was unarmed, all I could do was shout. Under water my yell became opaque but at the same time strident; the beast was unimpressed and continued moving toward Giorgio, slowly, confidently. (It takes too long to tell this; it happened in a few seconds.)

Giorgio heard my yell and turned quickly. The sudden movement frightened the man-eater, which changed its course and swam away. Even though he had had a good scare, Giorgio was busily taking picture after picture the entire time.

The scad on the bottom was still struggling and bleeding, so we felt sure the blue shark would come back. In twenty seconds it reappeared, intent on having some lunch. Apparently fearing that Giorgio was keeping him from his meal, it headed for him once more, menacingly—unlike any other sharks we had met.

This time Bruno thwarted the attempted attack by diving toward the shark and pointing his gun at him—a bluff, since the harpoon in that gun would have given no more than a needle-prick to the monster. Still, the shark was frightened and beat a retreat.

Giorgio and I exchanged looks that said 'Hurrah!' and he started to surface, turning to look at the madreporic wall, his back to the open sea. Our blue shark took immediate advantage of this mistake, coming straight for him again out of nowhere. Giorgio did not see him, Bruno was nowhere near, and I was helpless, unarmed. My stomach tightened, and I felt almost paralysed at witnessing the terrible threat to my friend. The shark was only a few yards away from his shoulder.

At that moment the discharge valve of Giorgio's auto-respirator expelled the air with a gushing sound, and a mass of bubbles completely hid him for a fraction of a second. Frightened out of its wits, the shark raced away and did not come back.

By that time, we began to feel that we knew a good deal about sharks. What were our tentative conclusions? Except for the last blue shark, not one of them had shown the slightest sign of living up to its fearful reputation. Most sharks, indeed, were more easily frightened than sardines, more fearful than any other fish we had seen or hunted. They appeared when other fish were wounded or in difficulty, waiting to get a meal with little trouble and little risk—not particularly inspiring behaviour, just like that of jackals and other scavengers.

But there are sharks and sharks, just as in the feline family there are cats, leopards, and tigers. If you kick a kitten, you run no risk. You can do the same thing to a baby panther. But it is inadvisable to give the same treatment to an adult one. We could not say that all sharks were innocuous, because there are hundreds and hundreds of species and we had encountered only a few, mostly of the non-anthropophagous variety. The man-eaters we had seen had perhaps not assaulted us because they are fish of the deep sea and did not feel at ease near the coast. We decided we would have to defer judgment on them. Some conclusions, however, we were able to make: that only a very small percentage of sharks may be considered dangerous; that most sharks are fearful and cowardly; that even the dangerous sharks will probably turn in flight when confronted by courage and intelligence . . . and luck.

7

Sea Devils

AFTER forty days of work in the Red Sea, we took stock of what
had been done and made a kind of interim report to ourselves.
We had some fifteen hundred hours of submersion to our credit
and were in remarkably good health. Dr. Grazioli, who had
kept scrupulously complete records of our physical conditions,
confirmed our own feelings by stating that the human organism
does not suffer at all from underwater work when it is undertaken as we had done it: with reasonable care and without
extremely long or deep immersions.

Some people might object to this statement by pointing out
that we had been specially trained for this work. But we could
point to Priscilla Hastings, who joined the expedition at the last
moment, who hardly knew how to swim, and yet quickly learned
to use air respirator, fins, and mask; she followed us during prolonged submersions, sharing our dangers and hard work without
any noticeable difficulty. One day I met her alone on the edge
of a coral barrier, painting the underwater scene with some
special pencils on parchment paper—forty feet down.

The scientific group had already collected hundreds of specimens, taken thousands of notes. The sports group had helped
collect the specimens and gained valuable experience in hunting.
The documentary group took pictures of all these activities, of most
of the fish, of plants and coral formations. We felt well satisfied
with the work we had accomplished to date, but more than ever
aware of how little we knew about the Blue Continent we were

exploring: its deserts, abysses, mountains, jungles, wolves and lambs.

We had become thoroughly accustomed to a different kind of life, a life under a different set of physical laws in a world of three dimensions, with a law of gravity that seemed strangely distorted. When one broke a hammer, for instance, the head sank down and the handle rose. We were used to living horizontally, remaining suspended, or perching in almost any attitude convenient for our work.

We were beginning to feel that the broader aims behind our expedition were not so Utopian as they might have sounded. We began to wonder, for instance, why fishing could not become something like animal husbandry. Animals that were once wild had been domesticated by man to supply many different food products on a steady, regular basis. Perhaps the same kind of thing could be done with fish—if good breeding methods and proper agricultural principles were adopted—as with herds of cattle and flocks of chickens. The entire fishing industry could be revolutionised, and men could increase their production of food from the sea a hundredfold, or more. Compare the savage's return from his hunting of wild animals with the production of organised ranches, and you see what could happen.

We were very interested in seaweed, too. With further study, we felt sure that these varied plants would prove of great value. We could picture the time when great fields of cultivated seaweed would be grown and harvested on the ocean floor—the work of a great and wealthy industry. As for mineral riches, everyone knows they are there in the sea. One day when we set off a small explosion to collect fish, we saw afterwards a long chain of bubbles which we learned were methane gas. Another time I came across a large yellow deposit of sulphur. The mineralogists need only to learn the use of respirators and fins to discover great deposits of coal, oil, and other valuable minerals in the Blue Continent.

Once when I was fighting against a very strong current deep in the sea, I had another idea. These currents are steady, strong, and may be found in thousands of places all over the world, only a short distance below the surface. Why not put specially designed turbines there to generate substantial amounts of power? We produce electrical current from our great rivers as they fall towards the sea. The sea itself has far more and greater rivers within it that are not being used. Ravelli told me that in Brittany there is a plant on the seashore that uses the currents in this way, which shows my idea is not completely fantastic.

We enjoyed talking about what might happen to a poor and desolate island in the Dahlak Archipelago when frogmen had accomplished their dreams. First, they would find many fresh-water streams gushing from the cliffs below the sea's surface. When that was piped above, one of the arid island's most serious problems would be solved. Next, underwater agricultural experts, working always without fear of sharks or other perils, would begin to cultivate in orderly fields the seaweed which one native had gathered to feed his flocks. Sheep, cattle, and other domestic animals would thrive, and feed and satisfy the people of the island.

Other experts, studying the habits and movements of fish, would increase by ten times the production of fish foods and fertilisers. Still others would harness the strong current of Nokra to make electric current. In a few years the men with the fins would have transformed the island into a healthy, prosperous, and happy place!

These were dreams, perhaps, but no more far-fetched than many others that have revolutionised the world and the ways of men. And they stimulated us to greater effort, sent us down into the depths with uplifted hearts and eager eyes. Always there was something new and rewarding to be seen.

Mantas, for instance.

It was seven o'clock in the morning, and the *Formica* was anchored about five hundred yards from shore. The sea was as smooth as glass, and there was not a breath of wind. We were getting our equipment ready for the day's work when we saw the black surface of the sea agitated by something. Then a fin appeared and disappeared—two fins together!

'Two sharks side by side!' someone said.

'Look how much water they displace!'

'They're gone—no, there they are again! Two sharks.'

'No—one very big one!'

There was only one way to find out. In a minute and a half, Bruno, Giorgio and I were in a boat rowed by Idris. As we went along, we put on our equipment, but then I found that I didn't have my mask. There was no time to return so, cursing, I resigned myself to staying in the boat. Bruno, armed with a gun, and Giorgio, with a camera, dived silently into the sea.

The water was very dark there, and I could not see the bottom, which was probably 100 to 125 feet down. But I could still see my friends advancing. Then the two fins emerged, retreated, turned toward them.

'Careful!' I shouted. 'They're coming toward you!'

Bruno's head came up a moment. 'It's a manta!' he shouted.

The manta and the two men approached each other. The beast then disappeared with Bruno and Giorgio chasing wildly after it.

'Mantas no good, manta bad,' grumbled Idris. He added that the mantas would not leave until the *Formica* left. Mantas loved to go under boats, he explained, and hook onto them and drag them away. They also fell in love with anchors and scraped against them affectionately with their horns. Since I had lost sight of my friends and the manta, I let Idris go on telling me some of the tales I had heard before about mantas and anchors.

In half an hour Bruno and Giorgio returned after a fruitless chase. Soon another boat came from the *Formica*, with Bucher, Grazioli, and Zecca, who wanted to go fishing. They slipped into the water, and in a few minutes I heard Zecca's voice, like the crack of a whip. 'It's here!'

Bruno, Bucher, and Grazioli hurried toward him, with Giorgio and me not far behind. But we were not in time to see Bruno, flashing past like a bolt of lightning, send his harpoon right between the two eyes of the beast. It rose up from the depths in a great leap—an enormous ray with big powerful wings and two 'horns' or fleshy lumps in front.

Zecca, who was above it, shot accurately, but his harpoon bounced off the manta's skin without piercing it. The monster writhed at the blow and headed for the bottom. Bruno was dragged down, until he released the gun, which was tied to a buoy on the surface. The buoy flew across the water as the manta fled at full speed. Unfortunately, the sounding line caught against Bucher's shoulders and tangled him up. He was in great danger of being dragged down, when the line suddenly broke. The manta swam away, dragging harpoon, spear, gun, and part of the line.

As with the barracuda and the sharks, the first round in our battle with the so-called dangerous fish had ended in its favour. But we felt that we would in time overcome the manta as we had overcome the others.

In the chase of the manta, many men were involved, and there was in the main a well-co-ordinated action against the fish, in spite of the fast sequence of events. This brings me to explain something about the language of the Blue Continent, the way underwater men communicate with each other. For the moment, I shall ignore Masino's mouthpiece for underwater speech, which is not universally adaptable and would be useless in the midst of great noise or at great distances. In general, we used the conventional signals of the Morse code for calls and danger signals. Sounds such as these travel very fast under water—at the rate of 1,340 miles per second, much faster than in air. But our principal means of communication was by precise signals agreed upon in advance. They were simple and easy to follow, as are the somewhat similar signs of directors in radio and television. And the comparison is not far-fetched, for many times I filmed pre-arranged scenes under water and had to have signs that would tell my 'actors' what to do.

No special language was needed to tell us that spring had come to the island of Dur Ghella in the Dahlak Archipelago. One night near the end of February a soft drizzle of rain came to the arid and barren island, so that by the next morning it was covered with many spots of green, with a few little yellow flowers, and the trees burst forth with buds. The day before, the only inhabitants of Dur Ghella had been sea gulls and sea hawks, which flew silently along the shore in search of food. Then with a noisy rush the swallows arrived on their return voyage to old Europe. With them came some quails and turtle doves. They went on their way, to be followed by pelicans and big black storks, which nested on the east side of the island, where cliffs plunged precipitously into the sea.

Cecco Baschieri, demonstrating remarkable ability as a mountaineer, climbed up on the rocks to spy on the love life of these birds—and to steal a pair of eggs, if possible. They were very rare, he said.

Speaking of eggs, we had a good quantity of scrambled turtle eggs for dinner every evening, just to keep up our morale. The fishermen from Yemen, who used Dur Ghella as a base, taught us to find them buried in the sand by probing with a long stick. That's how we discovered the little heaps, looking like beaten-up ping-pong balls, with their whites and yolks all mixed up inside. However they were quite edible.

During these days, the surface of the sea often seemed to be boiling because of the millions of sardines. One heard a patter that sounded just like rain and looked out to see thousands of sardines leaping from the water and falling back again. They too were in love, for spring had come.

The place was a paradise for native fishermen. Sampans from Yemen, Sudan, and Eritrea crisscrossed busily from all directions and made great hauls. At night the fishermen spread the sardines out on the sand to let them dry for several days. Then they put them in sacks and carried them to Jidda, Massaua, Hodeida. Two days later they were back again, scooping up sardines and drying them on the beach until there appeared to be dozens of little silver lakes—dead sardines—on the beaches.

Sardines, scads, and other nomadic fish were passing towards the north in shoals of tens of thousands. Behind them came sharks, masses of tuna, barracuda, and other pirates of the underwater world. The water's surface was broken by hundreds of triangular fins, and the moment of love for small fish coincided with the moment of death.

The fish that attracted the greatest attention with their complicated love ceremonies were the humped and voracious rhinoceros fish, which appeared by the hundred. They were so preoccupied with love that we found little difficulty in approaching and photographing them. You can imagine that fish which are so noisy about eating would make quite a turmoil over love. The water above them boiled. Underneath, their tails and brisk movements raised clouds of sand as particles of coral and madrepora were swept away in a kind of merry-go-round for boys and girls. In love-making, I noticed, they broke ranks and forsook military manœuvres, possibly because the sergeants were busy making love themselves.

Other inhabitants of the coral jungle were much more delicate about their emotional lives. The rays, for example, arrived in a long line—some black, some violet with blue circles, some yellow with little quills. They came in Indian file, with a large female in the lead and three, four, or five males behind—sometimes more. To the tip of the female's tail was attached the nose of the first male, and so on down the line, all of the giant creatures swimming at great speed with graceful flapping of streamlined wings. Occasionally one of the larger males took courage and, beating his fins a little faster than the others, passed the rest of the line and approached the female. If she accepted his proposal, she suddenly swam more erratically, flitted about, and then lay down on the sand for the act of mating to be performed.

If, however, the aspirant was deemed unsympathetic, the female manta altered her course and increased her speed slightly as the rejected suitor fell back to the end of the line.

I worked hard to get pictures of this great spectacle, but it was not easy to keep the mantas within focus. Then too, I was hampered by the fogginess of the water filled with clouds of plankton. The abundance of these microscopic morsels meant the presence of multitudes of fish of all kinds, however, giving work to Cecco Baschieri and his scientists from morning till night as they reaped a bountiful harvest for their collections.

Their collecting was aided by many different kinds of nets: plankton nets, shaped like funnels and with filters at the bottom; dragnets, with a special kind of stitch for slightly larger fish; and nets with batches of hoods suspended from a large float. The cases and aquariums of the Institute of Zoology were being filled quickly.

The Yemenite fishermen knew that this was the time for big catches, too. Their sampans were anchored at one end of the island, where the fishermen, working in groups of four, sang monotonous dirges as they worked, interrupted only by an occasional scream of anger as a shark stole a fish from one of the lines.

We anchored near by and watched. Each fisherman had a line about a hundred feet long, with a baited hook near the end. The last few feet of the line were wound round a stone which the Yemenite threw overboard. When it hit bottom, he jerked the line, freeing the baited hook so that it hung a little above the bottom. Then with rapid and graceful gestures, he worked the line, his hands running up and down so as to make the bait move and attract the prey.

With the few Arabic words that we knew and the few Italian words they knew, we talked a bit, and learned that round their sampans there were always many large sharks. So we decided to go beyond the breakwater where they fished, and try to photograph them in the deep as they stole fish from the hooks.

Gianni and I went out in a small boat the next day. The Yemenites greeted us warmly, but when they saw me slipping on my fins and the rest of my gear they cried out in a mixture of Italian and Arabic, with violent gestures, warning me of the terrible sharks I would run into. They obviously thought I was committing suicide.

Diving in the open sea, far from the coast, gives one a strange sensation. I could not see a coral bank or the bottom—only water. I felt very, very small and alone, with a constant premonition of danger behind me, causing me to turn round often to see what was there. And I found great clouds of plankton which cut my visibility to a minimum and increased my sense of being in the unknown.

The clouds of plankton, however, gave me the opportunity to observe a curious optical effect. The sun sends beams of light into the water which are broken up by the plankton particles into a kind of dense fog. Diving lower in an effort to get away from this fog, I looked up and saw the keels of the sampans with nets hanging far below them. Under the sampans, of course, there was a dark shadow, where the boats cut off the rays of light—a kind of dark cone extending toward the bottom. I swam into this cone of darkness and found that miraculously I could see quite clearly! The illuminated plankton created a fog that cut visibility, but in the area without light I could see as never before, as far down as twenty or thirty yards. It was like looking at something in the beam of a bright flashlight on a dark night. Into this clear cone of shadow, out of the bright fog, swam a lone angelfish, huge, perfectly round, and with a golden colour that gives it its name. Focusing my camera, I moved slowly down to film it.

After a short time I saw the nets of the Yemenite fishermen being pulled up, and then the friend I was waiting for appeared. A shark about seven feet long made a few tentative movements into the cone of darkness, evidently trying to see me better. I arched my back, gave a strong lunge, and shot quickly toward him to take my picture. He disappeared like lightning, so I surfaced. My mission was completed. I had filmed the nets, the unusual lights, the shark. There was no need to stay in the water, and anyway it is not very comfortable to have a shark beneath you. I jumped aboard the sampan, much to the relief of my Yemenite friends, who were sure that I had been eaten alive.

There were other interesting experiments and discoveries almost daily. In order to test the effectiveness of our curare harpoon, Cecco injected a dose of the poison, large enough to kill five oxen in a few seconds, into a still live and struggling cernia of almost seventy pounds. The curare had only one effect: that of a tonic. Even after several minutes when the cernia was put in the water, it darted away happily. We decided that curare could not poison fish.

Then we wanted to find out what effect different colours might have on fish. We sprinkled into the water at different places huge clouds of pigment, turning the water red, yellow, white. Some fish did not mind at all, did not seem to notice—especially the coral, butterfly, and other brightly coloured ones. The silvery fish fled quickly. The parrot fish seemed uncertain, slightly concerned but not frightened.

Even when the day's work was over, I took pictures, testing different lights, different colours. I filmed Priscilla Hastings as she sat painting sketches of some fish caught during the day. She always worked in the evening, sketching, or compiling the records for Baschieri. In the course of this she succeeded with impressive regularity in upsetting a little bottle of China ink, of which she fortunately seemed to have an unlimited reserve.

Our evenings were not always so peaceful and filled with such innocent amusements. During the nights spent on shore at some temporary island base, we sometimes had fights with crabs that lasted for hours. When the sun set, the sand round us became perforated with many little holes, from which crawled crabs with whitish faces and green feelers. Feeling not the slightest bit shy in our presence, they began to run round in all directions with a kind of grim playfulness. They were particularly attracted by shiny objects, the shiniest of which was the cover of my fountain pen. They stole it over and over again, and once I retrieved it at the edge of a hole, from the loving pincers of a very strong crab.

One night, a crab kept tickling the bottom of Gianni's foot while he was reading. After a time, Gianni went after the crab, which executed some brilliant manœuvres in eluding him. Roghi not only failed to catch the crab but succeeded in bumping against a box on which stood three glasses of boiling-hot tea—which fell in Priscilla's lap—and in shoving our cook just as he was putting salt in the soup—which did not improve the taste.

We began to cheer and place bets. The crab raced behind a tent, Gianni one leap behind it. We were sure the tent would collapse, but after five minutes Roghi gave up, a defeated man.

Two hours later we were going to bed. The carbide lamp was extinguished, and we were stretching out on our rubber mattresses. Suddenly there was an inhuman scream.

'Here it is! The cursed crab!'

The clever creature, lying between the mattress and the pillow, had celebrated the end of the day by biting the ear of a member of the National Underwater Expedition.

One morning, peaceful like most others, I took the greatest risk of all my time in the Red Sea. I did not realise it was a risk until later, for it did not concern anything like sharks, mantas, or octopuses. No, just a shell.

I was photographing Cecco as he worked among the madre-pore when I noticed a conelike shell about two inches across. I picked it up and tucked it under my swimming trunks. When we returned to the boat about an hour later, I showed it to Roghi.

'Look at the shell I found.'

'Drop it!' shouted Roghi. 'Drop it! Throw it away!'

I tossed the shell on the ground and looked for an explanation of Gianni's strange behaviour.

'It is a *conus textylis*—large and poisonous. It has a stinger inside that springs out to give one of the most poisonous stings of the tropical seas—usually fatal.'

I decided to limit my collecting to innocuous stamps in the future.

Another capture I made was more pleasantly memorable, chiefly because I am an explorer and not a hunter. It was a nurse shark—a little one, to be sure, but a shark. Such a capture is bound to be a great satisfaction for a non-hunter.

I had followed one strange fish with an elongated snout into a grotto about sixty feet down. Slipping my head inside to find out where it had gone, I saw not the fish I had chased but a big whitish shadow on the bottom. When my eyes grew accustomed to the dim light, I could make out that it was not just a big stone but something alive and moving slightly. It had a long slim body about five feet long, but I could not see distinctly enough to make out any details. Because of its whitish colour, I thought it might be an enormous sea eel, or some fish that lived in grottos that I had never seen.

I surfaced and called to those on the boat that there was something down in the water to shoot—a large, strange fish.

87

I congratulated myself on turning over to the hunters the job of hunting. But Roghi, who had come over in a small boat, handed his gun to me and conceded the 'game' to its discoverer.

Happily, I grabbed the long weapon, tied to float and harpoon, arched my back, and slipped into the water. On the way down, I wondered what kind of fish I would get and hoped it would be something interesting. I knew that my friends on the surface were already making wagers and waiting for my reappearance with nothing important so that they could all have a good laugh.

At the entrance to the grotto I looked inside. The whitish mass was still there. But where should I shoot it to kill it? I could not tell which was the head and which the tail, so I decided to aim at the centre. It was hard to put both the barrel of the gun and my head into the hole at the same time, but I finally made it. Then I pulled the trigger.

The whitish body threw itself into convulsions, and threw up clouds of sand inside the cave so that I could not see. Outside, I held onto the spear with both hands despite the terrific jerks on it. I had to keep the wounded creature from leaping out of its grotto while it still had so much fight in it.

The point of another gun and harpoon appeared at my side, and I felt grateful that someone had come to my aid. But why didn't he shoot? I took a quick look and saw no one, only a gun suspended there in the water beside me. Without trying to explain this fantastic apparition, I grabbed the second gun and fired again. By this time I was out of air and had to surface. Filling my lungs again, I returned below, grabbed the two spears, and pulled them out of the cave.

Then I saw my little shark, still fighting, and looking rather odd with its two long whiskers and a tail shaped like a flag. Blood was flowing from it freely, and it was some time before I managed to get it up and into the boat. Cecco congratulated me and thanked me for the new specimen. And Gianni explained the gun that magically appeared at my side. He had gone into the water to see how I was doing and realised that one shot would not be enough. So he had lowered down a second gun for me to use.

My adventure with the little shark was really quite insignificant compared with our encounters with mantas that occurred almost daily at that time. At Du Rig-Rig, one day, Vailati and Masino were out beyond the breakwater in a boat when they spotted two stupendous panther rays lying on the sandy bottom.

Bruno loaded his gun and dived. The rays disappeared at once. But when Vailati surfaced a few moments later he was calling out excitedly, 'A manta! I've shot it!' Apparently no sooner had the panther rays escaped than another ray came into sight and Bruno with a quick burst of speed had got close enough to use his harpoon before it too could get away.

The float, to which gun and harpoon were attached, started skimming over the surface of the sea like a motorboat, as the manta began its crazy chase to free itself from the weapon. Bruno jumped into the boat as Masino started the outboard motor and they took off after the float. Coming level with it, Bruno seized it and after some time and a great deal of work, succeeded in wearing the manta out.

Bucher, who had seen Bruno catch his manta, wanted to try his luck, so Masino took him to a likely spot. Raimondo entered the water and searched a long time, but was on the point of giving up since lunch time was approaching. Then he saw a manta advancing lazily about half-way down. Bucher could have dived straight down and fired his weapon, but he decided to experiment. He would descend below the beast so as to shoot it from below where the gills open, the most vital spot of any fish.

He carried out his plan perfectly, shot the manta from beneath, and watched it race away. The float skimmed over the water, with the boat in pursuit, but suddenly the float stopped and bobbed on the waves. The beast had succeeded in getting rid of the harpoon.

After recovering his weapon, Raimondo understood what had happened, and why one should not shoot a manta from below. The sounding line had pulled round and up, bending the harpoon and finally pulling it out of the animal.

Gigi Stuart, Cecco, and Roghi also caught a manta. They encountered a small school of the big creatures gliding along just below the surface as if warming their backs in the sun. They hit a two-hundred-pound fellow and eventually wore him out after quite a chase.

That was the expedition's fourth battle with mantas, two of them successful, but not one of them could compare with the manta dance one March night beyond the breakwater at Dur Ghella.

There was not a breath of wind, and the sea was smooth and endless, without a ripple. Some clouds rose from the horizon as the sun sank down and became a flaming red ball. I was in a boat with the scientific group, doing routine work, when Cecco saw something that stirred the flat surface some distance away. We started up the motor and headed for the spot, which turned out to be much further away than we thought. Fifteen minutes passed, and we were still a few hundred yards from the disturbance in the water.

Suddenly it stopped. Well, perhaps it had been only a school of sardines attacked by tuna or sharks. We were about to turn back when the surface of the sea was ripped open by a huge body leaping upwards with terrific force and speed. Spray poured over us, and we heard the sound of rain pelting down. All eyes were on a shiny spine, as black as India ink, hurling itself from the water toward the sky. At the peak of its flight, the creature elongated its blunt horns, spread its winged fins.

'A manta!'

The cry came from all our throats, as we grabbed the sides of the boat to save ourselves. For it had been set rocking violently by the beast's upward lunge.

We were in some danger, but we could not think of that. Here was a manta such as none of us had seen—truly a giant manta!

And how it performed! At the top of its leap, when it was almost vertical, it flipped itself backward, showing its white belly. Then with a resounding splash it toppled back onto the water, sending up another big wave and billows of foam.

Flipping its tail, the manta dived slantingly downward, still upside down and showing its white belly. Finally it disappeared from our view, and the boat stopped rocking. We spoke to each other in awed whispers, trying to estimate the size of the creature. Cecco decided that its wing spread was more than twenty feet, and we knew we had met one of the biggest of mantas.

Our talk was interrupted by another eruption about thirty-five feet away, but this time the manta was somewhat smaller. Its performance was almost identical, however: the upward leap, the backward dive, and the exit upside down.

The red of the setting sun tinted the clouds, the waves, the faces of the men in a small boat. The far-off islands turned dark violet. In this setting occurred the mass dance of the sea devils, the dance of the mantas of the Red Sea.

One after another they leaped, dived, splashed—one smaller, one larger, one quite near, one far away, and then two at a time, three at a time. We were in the centre of a sarabande of monsters, each one weighing several tons. Our position was precarious, but it was probably the only spot in the world in which one could witness such a spectacle; we remained, breathless, holding onto the boat, looking in all directions about us.

We dimly saw that the mantas were performing under water as well as above. We saw death-defying loop-the-loops, swooping speed trials, and dive-bombing.

But why were the mantas performing in this way?

After half an hour, when it began to get dark, something happened that gave us some idea of the meaning of the spectacle. We saw the surface of the water broken by rows upon rows of much smaller mantas, each about three or four feet across. In single file, they beat their little wings and scurried along the top of the water, leaving behind long streaks of foam.

They were baby mantas, the newborn!

We were perhaps the first in the world to see this fabulous and mysterious ceremony, to be in the very centre of a tumultuous gathering of these largest inhabitants of the tropical seas, the coming-out party of their children. At a certain moment in the manta's life, some mysterious force brings them together at one spot for the happy event. And we were there.

As if a signal had been sent up from the depths of the sea, the performance ended and the mantas disappeared.

8

The Phantoms of the Gubbet

AROUND Gubbet Mus Nefit, a seemingly endless bay of the Dahlak Archipelago, extends flat sandy land, almost level with the sea and absolutely deserted. One large and one narrow channel give Gubbet contact with the sea, and through the larger one the *Formica* passed to cast anchor in the bay.

In the Red Sea, the tides are violent and strong, with a considerable rise and fall. The channels act as valves for the loading and unloading of water in the bay. Four times each day great volumes of water pass through the channels, causing a rushing flood. Diving into the channel when the sea was moving, we used to feel ourselves dragged away as if by a strong mountain torrent. We sailed ahead at top speed in the midst of big and little fish, without a blow of the fins.

In the middle of the bay, at night, everything was calm. But no one on board could sleep because of the noise of an electric generator which fed current to a string of underwater lights. Most of us were at the rail observing this experiment to determine which fish were attracted by the lights and to see the nets of plankton caught by the scientific group.

Many interesting specimens appeared: tiny little fish whose external structures were transparent, making their internal structure visible, like certain plastic raincoats worn by girls who like to have their clothes seen. We saw little black-and-white crayfish, infusoria, and organisms no larger than specks.

93

All went into the jars of the scientific collection, with little cards specifying the date, place, and depth of withdrawal.

A lightning-like apparition broke the calm: a shark shooting toward the cone of light. We were used to sharks by this time, but the size and speed of this one evoked a cry of wonder. Just as quickly as it appeared it flashed away again. And despite my knowledge and belief concerning the nature of sharks, when I dived the next morning I kept remembering that vision and looked behind me occasionally.

Why did I go down in Gubbet Bay? To find a shipwreck— the wreck of a boat sunk about twelve years before. I thought it would be interesting to shoot some photographs of it or perhaps some scenes on its superstructure.

Our nacuda, who knows all about wrecks, gave careful navigational instructions based on sightings of a scrubby acacia and some white cliffs on the distant horizon. With this information Masino located it, and Giorgio and I descended. We poked about on the bottom for a while, not feeling too comfortable. The light was dim, but that was not the real reason. Probably it was the presence of a wreck, the atmosphere of death and destruction.

We slipped along the edge of the boat, seeing nothing but a dark wall. Finally we found the prow and under it the name painted in white letters: *Panaria*. I took a rapid turn round the old propeller blades, while Giorgio took several pictures. But we had no heart for our work and soon surfaced, to talk with our nacuda about the shipwrecks of Gubbet Mus Nefit.

Not one shipwreck, but many. In the bosom of the bay lay several ships, taking us back to a day in April twelve years before. Here was the last chapter of the story of the Italian Navy, caught in a trap in the Red Sea at the outbreak of World War II.

One night the silence of the bay had been broken by the roar of bombers. There was a sharp explosion, and the *Mazzini*, loaded with torpedoes, was hit squarely. The *Prometeo*, filled with naphtha, burned like an immense torch, as if in honour of its own name. For two days the flames burned, illuminating the end of the other sinking ships. The *Urania*, the *Bottego*, the *Sauro*, the *Panaria*—all lay stretched out on the bottom of the bay. Our nacuda, who had served the Italian Navy command and knew all about those events, pointed out to us the two dramatic masts of the *Sauro* poking up through the waves, and the rusted framework of the *Urania* lying on its side. These were the only remaining evidence of the vessels sunk in Gubbet.

The nacuda's tales of these dead ships of the Red Sea aroused our curiosity, and soon they were an irresistible attraction. The last remnants of the *Sauro* and the *Urania* seemed to beckon to us, inviting us to come below and see all. Finally, when a day came on which the waters of Gubbet had tossed away their fogs of plankton, we went in search of an extraordinary experience.

The prow of the *Urania* poked half out of the water. The rest lay on the bottom, pointing down abruptly toward the deep centre of the bay. The ship was on its side and seemed to be cut in two by the sea. A metal rail round the prow rose partly above the water, where it served as a comfortable perch for a white heron with a long neck, which seemed annoyed at our presence; below, it served as a pole round which little fish danced. The heron flew away with short sharp cries, cries that reverberated in a silence so deep that one could feel it. One could feel it because, round a dead ship, one is overwhelmed by the enormous mass so devoid of life; the smallest noise—the lapping of a wave against an iron plate, the rustle of the wind in the unsunk superstructure—rebounds and enlarges, making the long pauses in which nothing is heard seem empty.

We moored our little boat under the shadow of a helm that remained above the water. The immobile hub of the propeller, the blades of which were hidden, was pointed like a cannon towards the white sky of the Dahlak. One after another we put on our auto-respirators and entered the water—Bucher, Roghi, Giorgio, Enza, and I.

95

Other underwater explorers have encountered wrecks in their wanderings on the sea floor. They are not difficult to find, for example, along the Mediterranean coast. I had visited several and photographed two of them thoroughly: one in Sardinia at Cape Carbonara and one at Ponza. From these experiences, I expected the sunken *Urania* to be covered with soft greenish sea-weeds, all one colour, mimicking the colour of the sea; I expected deep shadows, dark inaccessible recesses, and an air of death.

The tropical sea, however, cannot conceive of the word 'death'. It wants to see life always flourishing with thousands of brilliant colours and in a multitude of forms—even in a metal body dead for twelve years. And that was what we found as we completed a marvellous voyage round the wreck, at depths of fifteen, thirty, fifty feet. The *Urania* did not remind me of any ship I had seen beneath the water. It was not empty; it did not disappear in the folds of sea-coloured seaweed. Thousands of fish populated it, fish of every size, shape, and colour—from the brilliant parrot fish to the fantastic arbalest, from the silvery, shimmering scad and *liche* to the slender barracuda. Never had the *Urania* entertained so many passengers and such lively ones.

Covered all over by a bright cloak of little corals, sponges, madrepore, sea urchins, oysters, the *Urania* was a formidable polychrome spectacle of yellow, green, red, black, violet, white, orange. We could not look at it and think of a shipwreck as a thing without life. The ship sank dramatically, lighted up with a great explosion. Since then, it had been covered with beautiful drapery, from the inside of its long smokestack to its first-class cabins.

Near the keel, huge steel plates that were broken at the time of the explosion and rusted since then by the salt sea waved back and forth, pushed by currents of water and giving the impression of the gills of a giant fish. That was how Giorgio and I slipped inside the *Urania*, calculating the space to the fraction of an inch and timing our movements to dart in when the plate swung widest. It was like passing under a huge guillotine with rough, but sharp, edges.

Inside, lights and shadows played through the rooms, the corridors, and in the large salon. We crossed mysterious openings, accompanied only by the sound of the air unloaded regularly from our auto-respirators. In the machine room, among the boilers, ladders, and pipes, square rays of light from far-off hatchways made topsy-turvy patterns.

I came to a black wall, in the centre of which a porthole showed the yellowish green water of the sea outside. Suddenly a face appeared in the porthole: Giorgio, exploring the next room. He was a phantomlike vision, a mask from which extended tubes and valves, two eyes dilated to see in the darkness, all framed by a hole studded with yellow sponges and shells of black oysters.

We found a passage and followed it together in a visit around the labyrinth, the last stop being in the bath, which was still intact. Occasionally the flash of a camera lit up the surrealist scene.

A mysterious gong kept sounding from somewhere, as if announcing the dinner hour, so we started looking for the dining-room. A winding passage carried us almost to the top, and we discovered the cause of the sound: one of the big metal plates that 'breathed'.

Then we heard a siren. We stopped, bewildered, and stared at each other. Its sound, distorted by the mass of water into something that reminded us of a phonograph record running down, still reached our ears clearly despite our disbelief. It really *was* the sound of a siren.

But not the siren of the wrecked *Urania*. It was the *Formica*, circling around the wreck to tell us that the sun was setting, that it was time to return. We had no idea that the time had passed so quickly. And suddenly we realised that we had not really paid any attention to our winding route through the wreck, that we did not know how to get back to the place where we had entered.

Seeing a gleam of light above us, we headed that way quickly, and emerged into a small, square mirror of water at the top of which was the sky. We were in a corridor that now went straight upwards through the ship. We came to the surface of the water, gulped some welcome fresh air, and saw that we could not escape that way. The walls continued straight up for some distance without anything to hold on to.

'Air?' I asked Giorgio, who in such matters is always more precise than I am.

'Enough for five or six minutes, I think.'

Waiting there would do no good, so we dived down again. The walls with their yellow sponges and little rose-red leaves of madrepore faded quickly as the light disappeared. We were not really frightened, but we were certainly beginning to feel uneasy. Inside the enormous framework, among tons of steel floors and walls, we could not imagine which direction we ought to take. With everything on its side, floor plans did not make much sense.

Through a crack we saw a little light, but it was a false alarm. There was no space for an exit.

We decided to go as deep as possible and look for those waving plates by which we had entered. As we descended, we breathed with great economy, hoarding the little air left us. Finally the plates were in front of us, but then a blood-chilling fact stopped us dead. They were no longer waving. They were not moving at all. The water currents which had moved them had ceased, and our trap doors were shut. The guillotine had fallen.

We could have gone back to the long corridor where there was air to breathe. But then we would have been trapped, and in going there would have used the last remaining air in our respirators. I had to try the impossible. I pushed against the big plate, braced my feet against a projection and pushed harder.

Against my expectations, it slowly moved—not much, but it moved.

I nodded to Giorgio, who darted through like lightning, streaking along the sand and scraping his back on the lower edge of the plate. I let the door swing shut, hoping that my friend outside would find some way to pull from there. With my heart in my mouth, I watched a line of light on the sand at the bottom to see if it grew wider. Two seconds, three seconds, four seconds.

The big plate moved, began to open. Clever Giorgio had found a way to brace himself and was pulling with all his might. I crouched low and at the first possible moment slipped through.

The nightmare was ended. We sped for the surface, gulped in fresh air, and signalled to the boat to pick us up.

That night I had a hard time going to sleep. I kept seeing scenes from inside the wreck, and my thoughts finally turned to a comparison of my experience with that of the old type of diver in heavy suit and with a hose of air from above—the kind of diver who works on wrecked ships.

Theirs is considered a highly hazardous profession, and they have many accidents. I believe they are caused in most cases by the clumsiness of their equipment. The hose that brings the diver air, the cable that hoists and lowers him, forces him to undertake difficult gymnastics to enter the interior of a ship, bars him from many places, and continually threatens him with entanglement. He cannot possibly assume a horizontal position, which is the best way to enter cracks, portholes, and wrenched doors.

One of the most common accidents to these divers occurs when he is inside a ship and there is a swelling of his suit because of an excess of air sent down from the surface. He rises like a balloon, hits against the ceiling, and is almost helpless, unless he can let out some of the air through the rubber wrists of his suit.

Another great peril is presented by the hundreds of little

projections, sharp and curved pieces of metal that abound on a wrecked ship, each one capable of cutting the suit, which results in the diver losing all his air and drowning.

On top of all this, there are the great precautions that the diver must take to decompress himself and reduce his suit pressure to that at the surface when he comes up, in order to avoid blood embolisms. Consequently, only a very few divers—you can count on one hand all those in the world—can push beyond 100 or 125 feet in their work, in spite of the complicated equipment and a special ship of assistance. If they could descend easily beyond these limits, some of the great riches of the world beneath the water would be open to them. There are scores of wrecked ships all over the world, lying between one and two hundred feet deep, containing great treasures.

Our advice, after our experience, is that divers should become agile amphibians, equipped with fins, masks, and individual respirators, instead of weighted, restricted automatons. Then they can go almost anywhere in the Blue Continent, not only with ease but with pleasure.

9

The High Seas

AT first we could not believe that Benedetto was a Sicilian fisherman and not an Arab. He came aboard the *Formica*—thin, tall, his face deeply lined, dressed in a *futa*, and barefoot—looking no different from the thousand other natives of the Dahlak.

Then we saw that he was truly Sicilian. We saw the cunning in his flashing eyes, heard his unmistakable accent. He had spent twenty out of his fifty years at Dahlak. He had been married just a few days before his departure from Sicily on a long fishing trip, and had thought he would go back just as soon as he earned a little money. At the end of every fishing season since then, Benedetto had decided to go back to Sicily, but he never got farther than Massaua, for the simple reason that he spent all his money there. Then he had to go back to the islands and start all over again.

We concluded that he talked about going back to Sicily only from habit. He seemed to be happy as the admiral of a little flotilla of fifty native fishing boats. Possibly the drops of Arab blood in his veins, dating from the ancient Arab invasion of Sicily, had somehow brought him home, and he found it impossible to leave.

He came on board the *Formica* to discuss with Bruno a possible trip round the edge of the Dahlak Archipelago. We wanted to push into the islands and shoals of the high seas, where Baschieri's men could gather additional specimens of marine life, where the sun beats with its full force, where the strongest currents flow and where the greatest number of migratory fish pass. The sports group wanted to hunt for even larger creatures, and take part in more exciting adventures. And we documentarians longed for more worlds to film, to add a new chapter to the expedition's history. Finally, we knew that in the high seas we could extend our studies of the shark—the special quarry of all three groups. Up to that time we had encountered about a hundred sharks, some of them anthropophagous. Despite the old adage that 'the sharks of the Red Sea are the most dangerous on the globe', we had found them to be easily intimidated. If the statement were really true, our experiences meant that amphibious men could work without real peril anywhere in the world. But we hesitated to make flat statements on this subject. Someone might argue that the sharks we met round Dahlak were smaller than most, of a less aggressive nature, living as they do in peaceful channels. Perhaps the true shark, the shark of terrible legend, was the shark of the open sea. We wanted to find out.

So the *Formica* headed south, picking up on the way some of the scientific group that had been working at our first headquarters in Dissei. It was good to see this place again, where I had encountered my first shark and done my first important filming of the Blue Continent.

Benedetto advised us to stop long enough for a look at a little island that rises sharply in the open sea, between Dahlak and the Buri peninsula, an island called Sehil. We had been there only a short while when we saw a spectacle worthy of Benedetto's promise.

Gigi was in the water when he saw a squadron of tapering barracudas arriving from beyond the breakwater and curving towards Cecco, some distance away. They were somewhat different from the usual type, being shorter and with a different shape of mouth. But they were three feet long, and there were hundreds of them. They passed Cecco and shot under our feet as we dived to meet them. If they had wanted to attack us, they

Enza Bucher with a freshly caught sea eel six-and-a-half feet long.

A startled pigfish which, like many creatures of tropical seas, has a horny, beaklike mouth for grinding Madrepore and coral, its principal food.

Bruno Vailati with a rare specimen of Red Madrepore
found at a depth of 120 feet.

The cobra fish, whose deadly sting claims the lives of many
pearl fishers. Its protective color changes are shown in these
two pictures, where it first hides among the brownish green
clumps of Madrepore, then blends with the yellowish background. Near the surface it turns blue to match the waters
of the sea.

From a small coral grotto an « Aragosta » lobster faces a human intruder. At the left is a Star Madrepore, suggesting a snowflake seen under a microscope.

Two views of the same subject, showing how deep water filters out red and yellow, leaving everything azure blue. The first picture was taken with natural light, the second with a flash bulb.

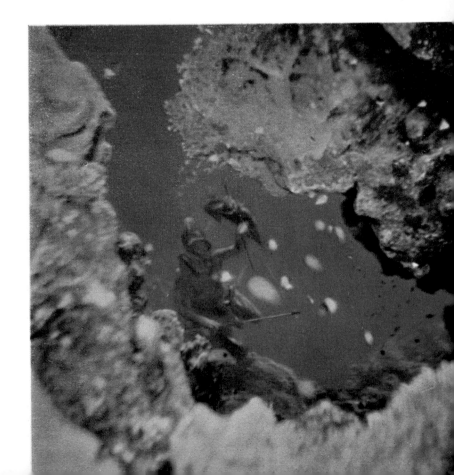

These fish were caught in nets by the expedition's Scientific Group, but many rare specimens were eaten by larger fish before they could be hauled in.

A manta leaving a cloud of blood behind after being
harpooned by Raimondo Bucher.

would have left nothing but bare skeletons in a few seconds, but the idea fortunately did not enter their heads.

According to Benedetto, these gentlemen had quite a different attitude toward the local fishermen, who often stand in water up to their waists as they pull in their nets. The barracudas cause a great deal of trouble, biting the fishermen's legs. This brings up the matter of 'psychological superiority' of amphibious man over dangerous fish, a superiority that normal men apparently do not have. With their heads above the surface, the fishermen not only fail to see the danger approaching but have nothing with which to combat it. The barracudas, satisfied that they are dealing with defenceless creatures, rush to the attack.

We, on the other hand, see them coming and go to meet them. A simple motion of counter-attack is enough to put them to flight. Baschieri found himself right in the middle of a large group of them and, seeing a particularly beautiful specimen, shot it. His attack against one of their number did not annoy the others. Instead, it made them flee even faster.

The next day, I was down in the water with Giorgio when he informed me, through the sign language of the Blue Continent, that numerous sharks of respectable dimensions were approaching. We promptly sat down on the bottom, waiting for them to come along so that we could photograph them. In the silence that was broken only by the gurgle of air bubbles from Giorgio's apparatus and the sound of my own breathing, we calmly anticipated our rendezvous with the sharks of the high seas—an incredible adventure that I would have found hard to believe if I had not been present.

Suddenly a shark appeared, passing rapidly in front of us. He was of the dangerous dark variety, about twelve feet long. Right behind him came two timid blackfins, followed by another just like the first. The blackfins circled at some distance, obviously afraid of us, but the big dark fellow began almost at once to make very quick passes at us. We were really quite pleased at the chance to get such good pictures, and ground away on our cameras. We felt less comfortable, however, when we noticed that the timid blackfins, stimulated by the aggressive actions of their larger companion, began to threaten us, too.

A man attacked by a wolf can defend himself with a big stick, but when a wolf has companions, the animals gain courage from each other and they all attack together. We were frightened, but at the same time pleased to experience this initiation into the ways of sharks of the high seas.

The big shark turned and headed straight for Giorgio, who had his eye to the view finder trying to catch the 'stampede' of the beasts, at least at the beginning. He obviously had not even thought of what he would do in the later stages of the attack. This time the big shark really meant business and kept coming at Giorgio, who used the only weapon he had: the camera. Lifting the heavy machine by its two handles, he beat it with all his might against the shark's snout. It was a powerful blow, but the shark was probably more startled than hurt. At any rate, it turned and raced away, with its two friends tagging along behind.

With our hearts pounding, we surfaced, to find Masino shaking his head in wonderment. He had just arrived at the spot and had seen the climax of the scene. With his hand he signalled, 'You had a narrow escape that time!'

The sharks around the Dahlak would never have had the courage of our aggressive dark friend in the open sea. Still, it had run away when man counter-attacked. We began to wonder if there was a fundamental difference between sharks from different localities. Only further experiences would tell us.

Late that afternoon, Gigi Stuart harpooned a most unusual specimen. We were having a little snack on the boat, stretched out comfortably in the last rays of the sun after our long immersions, when Cecco saw a large pelican about fifty yards away. This clumsy bird with a beak so huge that it looked ridiculous even on a pelican, sat on an overhanging rock almost above us.

'I'm sorry, Priscilla,' Cecco said to his artist-assistant, who was always upset at seeing birds shot, 'but this beautiful catch is mine.' He brandished his gun and shot, but the rocking of the boat spoiled his aim. The pelican rose in flight, but seemed to be either very tired or not very worried, so circled round and settled in the water not far from us. Glaring at us watchfully, it swam between us and the shore.

'This is my moment,' Gigi said. 'Keep quiet.'

He put on his fins and mask, grasped his gun, and slipped silently into the sea. As he swam toward the pelican, the big bird began to toddle away, wondering where to go. There were rocks on one side, the boat on another. Then Gigi went under the water completely, baffling the pelican, which seemed to know that there was danger near by but could not understand it.

Gigi was beneath the bird, with the idea of shooting it in such a way that it would be only slightly wounded and thus could be captured in good condition. His plan worked perfectly.

From the boat, we saw the pelican leap, beat its wings, and fall to the water again. Gigi emerged and, despite the pecks, kicks, and blows from the bird's wings, held it firmly until we came up with the boat. His shot had just grazed the wing, and the pelican was still in good health. From that time on, the *Formica* had a new mascot.

Going south from Sehil we passed near an island of similar name—Dehil—where some of us would have liked to land. It was Benedetto who told us about it early one morning as he came into the cabin and awakened me by pulling on my leg, which stuck over the end of the berth about ten inches. I suspected that he was pulling my leg figuratively, too, in the story he told, but he swore it was true.

'Dehil is inhabited only by women,' he said, 'young and beautiful, old and ugly. They are Arabs with fair skin and blue eyes, the most beautiful of the race.'

'Are we going to land?' I asked, trying not to look too interested, but actually wide-awake and ready for a new kind of exploration.

'No,' said our chief, Bruno, almost too quickly. 'There are no good depths here.' I wondered why he had to measure everything by metres only, then listened to the rest of Benedetto's story.

'The women fish most of the day, for trocas, the mother-of-pearl shell. The old ones stay at home and work the same shells, making them into beautiful things. Their beauty and their skill in fashioning mother-of-pearl are well known around the Red Sea, so occasionally sampans land to conclude business of a two-fold nature,' Benedetto smiled the smile of a good Sicilian. 'If the quality of the merchandise offered, the mother-of-pearl, is satisfactory, the first transaction is concluded. If the other merchandise is equally good, that is if the sailors satisfy the young Arabs with the blue eyes, then the second transaction is also concluded.'

Thus the women live on their island in sacred peace without the quarrels of married couples. The fathers will never be seen again, and the mothers will not remember them two days after the transaction. But the race at Dehil is perpetuated. We looked at the rocky island that was slipping away behind us.

'What about the boys born there?' I asked Benedetto.

'They stay on the island until they are seven or eight years old. Then they are put on the first sampan that appears, and they learn to be sailors.'

And that is the truth, according to Benedetto.

We came to the island of Madote, where Silverio Zecca had a great day. At the base of a coral precipice, he saw a gigantic brown umbra, a big-bellied fish with its mouth always half open. This one was of a very inviting weight so, thinking more about a good dinner than glory, Zecca dived toward the fish. Just as he was about to shoot, he saw a large shadow on his left. Forgetting about the umbra, he crouched and turned slowly so as not to frighten this more interesting prey. Propped against a huge brain coral and seemingly stuck to the coral wall, there was a huge turtle. It seemed to be sleeping, but when Zecca pointed his gun, the turtle leaped and headed for the bottom, swimming jerkily but very fast.

This was his undoing, for Zecca found himself in a good position to shoot the beast squarely in the neck. The turtle struggled, Silverio tugged on the sounding line, and the water turned red with blood. But the hunter had come down without a respirator, and he was almost out of breath. Holding the line, he quickly surfaced, but before he could descend again the line was jerked violently and then went limp. The turtle had freed itself from the harpoon.

From above, Raimondo Bucher saw the beast emerge from a cloud of blood in his flight. But the turtle was swimming slowly and apparently without direction. So Raimondo dived and grabbed one of the turtle's back legs with both hands, but could not bring it up alone. Zecca, with a lungful of fresh air, went down again in time to see Bucher being dragged away; he caught the other leg and together they brought the turtle to the boat. It was large and thrashed about a lot, so instead of trying to get it in the small boat we dragged it to the *Formica*, where it was hoisted aboard with the aid of a tackle.

That was not the end of Silverio's day, however. He re-entered the water and eventually caught up with Masino and Giorgio. The latter had seen a stupendous butterfly fish with yellow and violet stripes and was searching for it in a cave beneath a great mass of madrepore. Finally he saw it—terribly frightened—at the entrance to a crevice. Giorgio advanced and looked inside. The butterfly fish was nowhere to be seen, but there was another fish: a great whitish shadow like the one that had once puzzled me. It was a nurse shark, simple-minded and harmless, but very big.

Giorgio shot to the surface and called Zecca and Masino, then took them down to show the exact location. But the shark did not allow himself to be pointed out for the kill. Already perturbed by the first meeting with Giorgio, it decided to flee when it saw the fish-man reappear. With a flash it stirred up a cloud of sand and raced out of the little cave. Giorgio leaped out of the way, but a flip of the immense tail hit him, knocking away his mouthpiece and filling the mask with water. Although he had to surface at once, he saw Zecca take out after the fleeing shark, which soon darted into another cave.

In a few minutes, the three men floated down above the opening of the cave, after formulating a plan of attack. The beast had slipped into a cave with two entrances, one large and one narrow, so Masino took up his station at the narrow entrance, with his camera, while Zecca approached the main crevice with his gun. Giorgio stayed behind to film the whole scene.

As Silverio approached the entrance, the shark made another effort to escape. But this time his adversary had a gun which put a harpoon right in its gills.

The beast twisted and beat its fins furiously, but Zecca dragged it from the cave without fear and pulled it toward the surface. All alone he was handling a fish twice his size, at least—a wounded creature flipping its tail with great power, writhing in an effort to seize its attacker in the big mouth, which kept opening and closing. The shark could not overcome Zecca, who kept pulling it steadily toward the surface. We saw the figures of the shark and the underwater man gradually rising, two figures intertwined, struggling, actually bound together by the turns of the sounding line as well as the lines of the harpoon and gun. The conqueror and the conquered came up together, but it was the shark that lay expiring in the bottom of the boat.

There was much talk about Silverio's two catches. The shark was the largest of that variety that had been captured, and the turtle was six times as big as any we had seen at Dahlak. Baschieri was beside himself with joy, chiefly because of the turtle shell that would enrich his collection so much. We documentarians were in good humour, because we had filmed two spectacular scenes. It was a good day, all round, thanks to Zecca.

Southern Islands and Atolls

AN atoll is an island that did not have enough force to rise above the surface of the waves and so remains forever submerged in a few feet of water. Looked at from the floor of the Blue Continent, it is a gently sloping hill compared to the mountains we call islands.

The Mugiunia atoll, where we stopped for some exploration, did indeed give the impression of a lovely, peaceful hill. Enormous madrepore were its vegetation. The atmosphere around it was light-green water, averaging thirty feet in depth. It was very quiet.

I decided to have a look round before taking the camera under water. Submerging a few feet from the boat, I saw Enza Bucher looking intently at a school of scad. She dived, fired, and hit one, which struggled fiercely, with great loss of blood, while she was trying to bring it to the surface. As a result, four sharks appeared almost at once, quite interested. I did not take much notice of them at first but went to help her carry her prey to the boat as quickly as possible. The four dangerous visitors circled widely round near the bottom, searching for the wounded fish whose blood spread through the water.

Suddenly one shark discovered that the scad was no longer near the bottom, but was being pulled toward the surface. He pointed his snout toward us, then hesitated a moment in surprise at having found two big meals instead of one small one. But only for a moment, after which he flew straight up at us. Enza gave a sharp cry and drew up her legs. I did the same, but at the shark's arrival I kicked out at his nose with both feet, which were shod conspicuously in red fins.

Who can tell what they must have looked like to the shark? At any rate, he didn't like the idea. He changed direction quickly, skimmed along the surface ten feet from us, cutting it with his dorsal fins, then headed for the depths and disappeared. Then I helped Enza bring home her scad.

At Mugiunia I had an unforgettable encounter with a *liche*. I called it Mariuccia because of a great resemblance to my aunt, and this is not just a joke. If you talk with any underwater men, you will find that many fish down below remind them strongly of people they know. Cheena, sargus, mullet, and others sometimes have the physical traits of a high-school German teacher, a bicycle racer, Toscanini, or a dear relative. This is not meant to be insulting. I was completely serious in thinking that the *liche* looked like Aunt Mariuccia.

Finning along about forty feet down, grazing enormous sheets of madrepore, I was looking for subjects to film. After rejecting an ordinary cloud of bonitos and some black arbalests I had photographed many times, I came upon Mariuccia. She was a beautiful silver *liche* weighing about ninety pounds, measuring about five feet, and as flat as the shield of a medieval warrior. I pressed the lever that starts the movie camera, and the whirring sound reverberated through the depths. The fish made a sudden start, and I was afraid it would flee like all the others. But no— the buzz of the camera enchanted it. Its big round eyes softened as it began to rock back and forth slightly, careful to keep within the frame of the camera. Sweetly and demurely, it moved closer to the camera, so I had a chance to observe it carefully as I filmed. A little blue fish with a yellow belly, about the size of a finger nail, swam alongside it—it was an excited parasite, very excited, darting nervously about. When Mariuccia opened her gills to breathe, the little fish made nibbling thrusts inside, moving in, taking a tiny bite—I could actually see a fleck of blood—and moving out before the gills closed.

I had seen comparable relationships many times. One of the most amusing occurred when Masino was filming a ball fish which was assaulted by four of these tiny parasites. They threw themselves against the fish, chewing its fat white belly and making it jump from the pain and dash away in headlong flight.

My friend Mariuccia was somewhat troubled by the little parasite, but in this situation decided to pretend that it did not exist.

After photographing the *liche* in all attitudes, the camera showed me that I had run out of film. I had to surface and load again. I did not believe, of course, that I would see Mariuccia again. But there she was a half hour later, floating peacefully about six feet beneath the keel of the boat.

To reward such faithfulness, I called Silverio Zecca, who was passing about thirty feet away, and signalled for him to notice the *liche*. He understood, so I aimed the camera and started it turning again. Mariuccia, enchanted once more by the buzzing sound, passed slowly in front of me. Behind her, I saw Silverio, aiming his gun. With a metallic sound the arrow flew and centred itself in the target. The big fish jumped and started through a series of crazy evolutions, which finally enabled it to pull the harpoon out. I continued filming the scene, even when Mariuccia fled like a rocket.

I thought that the story was finished—another tale which pointed out the dangers of young beauties taking movie tests. But an hour later, there was a *liche* in front of my camera. Was it another one? No, it was my Mariuccia for I could see the big wound in her side. Vanity had conquered fear, and she was ready for another 'take'. And this time, I did not call Silverio.

After stopping at the tip of the Buri peninsula, which juts

out into the open sea, at the two Asheker Islands and a pair of unnamed shoals, we went even further south to the island of Shumma. There, Gigi Stuart prepared a bomb so that the scientific group could collect a quantity of small fish and the rest of us could study the sharks that would quickly gather. Shumma is situated between Africa and the Dahlak, in a very deep channel along which many ships pass. The sea promised to be full of sharks and many other fish.

The boat was at the edge of a coral barrier when Gigi busily inserted the detonator in his red package of 'plastic' explosive. Everyone was waiting eagerly, for it is important to get into the water quickly after an explosion. Gigi touched his cigarette to the short fuse and tossed it toward the water. Priscilla closed her eyes as the little bomb sank toward the bottom with several curious fish making gay turns about it.

There was a strong blast, a reverberating echo, and the sound of hundreds of fish falling back into the water, followed by the sound of more hundreds farther away, leaping from the sea as a result of the after-effects of the explosion. For an instant, the sea was changed from blue to silver. Within ten seconds we were all in the water—even Priscilla, despite Cecco's warnings about tiger sharks. Priscilla could not have been kept out of the water at such an exciting time by ten tiger sharks.

Giorgio and I went down with our respirators and sat back to back at the base of the barrier. For a while we looked at the scientists hard at work above, collecting their little fish. Then we saw large dentexes with long faces, and whitish cernias peeping out from the crevices in the rock. Rather hesitatingly, they swam out and started circling, then caught sight of some dead umbra with bellies turned to the sky, which they carried away hungrily.

Quickly the scene became repopulated. Barracudas arrived in schools. Then out of the corner of my eye, I saw a dark mass advancing from the left. The first of the sharks were coming, zigzagging across the bottom. The first one felt that he lacked a little courage, so waited for three others to catch up with him. The fourth attracted our immediate attention, for it was a beautiful beast—large, long, and chubby. We decided it was a mackerel shark, about ten feet long and with a healthy set of teeth, which we saw when he exposed them in chewing a dying parrot fish.

A flash bulb exploded! Clever Giorgio—he had caught a picture of the shark having a snack—a snack that was not altogether enjoyable because of the disturbance of the flash.

The fish departed, and the stage before us was empty again.

We shifted a bit towards the breakwater, and I saw one of the four sharks—not a very large one—turn courageously toward the scientific group. Gigi saw it, too, and dived, while the shark slowed down before three or four fish killed by the bomb, undecided which to eat. The hunter then executed one of the best 'approaches' I have ever seen, sliding along the rocks almost imperceptibly, freezing when the shark turned towards him. But he had bad luck. Just as he was about to aim, his gun barrel hit the coral. At the sound, the shark darted away.

If Gigi had bad luck, so did the shark. He fled to a spot right under the legs of Cecco Baschieri who, seeing a shark in perfect position, pulled the trigger and hit the beast in its most vital spot, right behind the gills. The spear even came out on the other side.

Blood flowed all around; there was a tense but brief struggle, and then the shark was captured. In little more than one minute I had captured on film a drama filled with emotions: cunning, fear, courage, surprise, decision, agony.

Giorgio and I resumed our interrupted trip beyond the breakwater, but suddenly we stopped. Below us in the water there appeared to be an airport—an airport eighty-five feet down, with a dozen planes ready to take off. They were mantas dozing on the sand.

We filmed them as they lay there, but wanted to take them in flight. I made all the noise I could, but they continued their naps undisturbed. While Giorgio aimed his camera, I swam up behind them, thinking they would certainly take off when I came near. But nothing happened—even at six feet, three feet, one foot. I was right next to the first one, so reached out my hand and touched its tail. It jumped, shook jerkily, then shot upwards, with the others following. The beating of the big wings stirred up so much sand that I could not see, but the cloud round me was suddenly lighted by a streak of lightning, and I knew that Giorgio had taken his picture.

At the same moment, at the other end of the island, Zecca had come upon a school of mantas, had separated one from the others, and shot it. Despite a violent struggle, he had conquered it alone with intelligent use of an 'elastic' technique: giving a great deal of line to the beast to tire it out. Finally, he hoisted his manta aboard the boat.

The final adventure of the day involved Cecco, Gigi, a scad, and a shark. The scad was travelling along peacefully enjoying the last rays of the sun. Suddenly there appeared ahead of it two fish the likes of which it had never seen before. They came toward it, but, before it understood that Messrs. Stuart and Baschieri were not fish but men who intended to eat it fried that very evening, a spear of steel had penetrated its body. Gigi was then struggling with the scad when a large shark sprang out of the shadows right by his feet. For several seconds, man, shark, and prey crisscrossed in underwater manœuvres. The shark showed no fear of Gigi, nor was it intimidated when Cecco intervened with actions intended to frighten the beast. Such moments of fear and courage add to the store of our knowledge about the actions of sharks. But no one could explain why suddenly, for some reason of its own, the beast went away. The dinner, captured at such a price, was carried to the boat.

Later that week, Shumma gave the expedition another unforgettable day. Early in the morning we were at work with the sports group. Vailati, Bucher, Enza, and Zecca were with us—or rather above us. Masino and I were on the bottom with respirators and cameras, ready to film a hunting scene.

At first it seemed that Shumma wished to place a curtain between us at the bottom and the others on the surface. Dense clouds of parrot fish passed by with the current, interrupting the rays of the sun and making all fish look like silhouettes, except for the fins and tails, which were transparent, yellow, and strongly illuminated. And around each figure there seemed to be a halo of light. My eye at the view finder sought to capture on film glimpses of this overflowing richness. Then the masses of fish separated as Bruno and Zecca swam toward me, and Raimondo and his wife toward Masino—cutting through the living curtain that had separated us.

We followed them, ready to turn the cameras. Large fish of many kinds had come to visit us at last, with good-sized sharks and mantas among the first. It looked like a promising day.

The mantas circled round us in groups, appearing and disappearing in the depths. Bruno aimed and hit one of the largest, which immediately found great strength in its wounded body and jerked Bruno violently. The gun flew out of his hand and the creature sped away.

Giorgio enjoyed the panorama a great deal. He was about a hundred yards away and had scarcely slipped his head under water when he saw below him a manta which flew past like a rocket, dragging behind it a harpoon, a long sounding line, and a gun without an owner.

Before he could say 'Tch!' Bruno arrived, finning like mad and cursing. By signs he asked if Giorgio had seen a manta and which way it had gone. Giorgio signalled, 'Ahead and to the left,' and Bruno took up the chase.

Not far away, Masino had seen another group of mantas crouching on the bottom. He approached them cautiously to get pictures, being very careful not to disturb them. But suddenly the winged devilfish rose and fled, and in a moment Masino saw what had upset them. Above were fifteen or sixteen large tortoises—an amazing sight, for we had never known them to travel in such large groups. Masino, delighted at having fallen out of the frying pan into the fire, got a beautiful shot of the majestic passage of the tortoises.

At just about that time, I was filming Zecca's capture of a beautiful ray. Bruno returned to action with a new gun and went off to seek his revenge on the mantas.

These fish reappeared some time later in a group. They swam lazily, in formation, parallel to the coral barrier. Obviously the shots of Bruno and Silverio had not overmuch disturbed them. They almost flaunted their imperturbability. Without a word, Bruno, Silverio, and Bucher threw themselves into the formation. This time there were three shots and three mantas to be hauled into the boat.

Masino and I were still in the water and, as we hoped, the large amount of blood from the devilfish attracted many sharks. Three of them repeatedly came near us with quick thrusts, and we were happy at being able to photograph them to our heart's content.

The next day I was filming a sea anemone, with its green tentacles and fleshy red body, and getting a good close-up of a pomacentrid, or damselfish, cleaning up its deadly friend. I saw Masino climb astride a big brain coral to take pictures of me filming the sea anemone.

In half a minute, I noticed that Masino had stopped his shooting and seemed to be staring at something behind me. Suddenly he shook, waved his arms, moved his fins, and acted as if he were seized by an epileptic fit.

Confused and somewhat frightened, I moved a bit, and felt

behind me a violent blow and a sudden displacement of a great deal of water. Turning round, I saw a little shark about five feet long diving toward my legs. I kicked out, the shark fled, and we surfaced.

Masino explained that while I was kneeling, the shark had come quite close, unafraid because we were not moving. At first he shot the scene, but when he saw the shark coming nearer and nearer, he was worried. Finally, with the shark breathing at my feet, Masino had made his violent movements. Perhaps it had only wanted to sniff my feet. Sharks can be very impudent.

A short time later a much larger shark became courageous enough to approach Bucher in the water, but it ran into a sharp harpoon instead of someone's feet; Raimondo had another prize.

In a few more days we left Shumma. Since we had found so many sharks there, why did we go away? For the same reason that we had left every other spot at which we worked. Even the richest waters gradually became depopulated after we had been diving a while. The time came when coral fish were the only creatures remaining. Mantas, sharks, rhinoceros fish, tortoises, barracuda—all had departed for other regions. It was obvious that word spread round quickly among fish about danger zones, which soon became 'off limits' for most of them.

This proves that fish have a genuine capacity for quick and intelligent reactions. And it is not just individual reactions but collective ones. To most human beings, fish seem the most isolated, the most 'shut up in themselves' and the least endowed with collective organisation of any living creatures. But they regularly make important decisions together—even those belonging to different families and species.

The scientific group was particularly pleased at being able

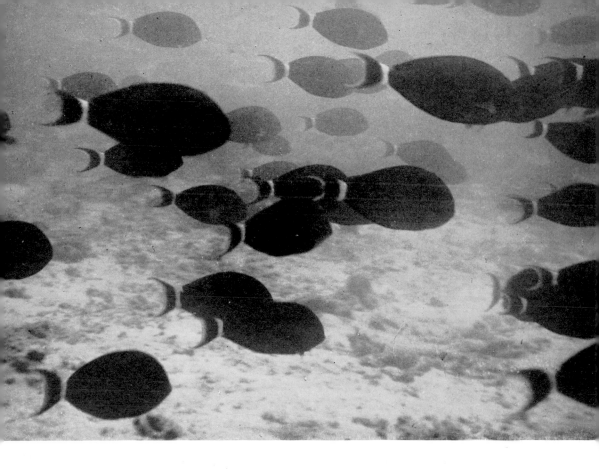

Above: Some of the smaller inhabitants of the Red Sea, a school of 'crossbow' fish. Below: a pair of sharks.

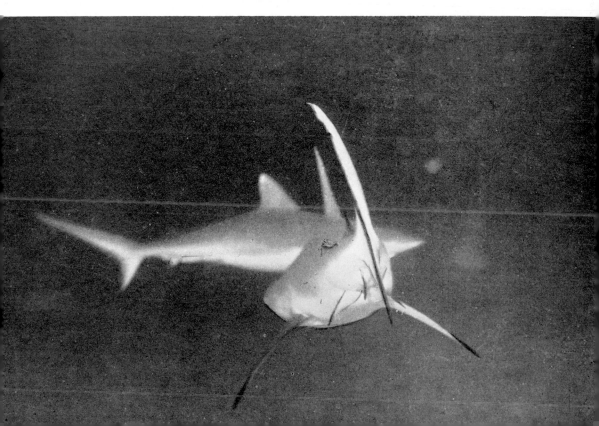

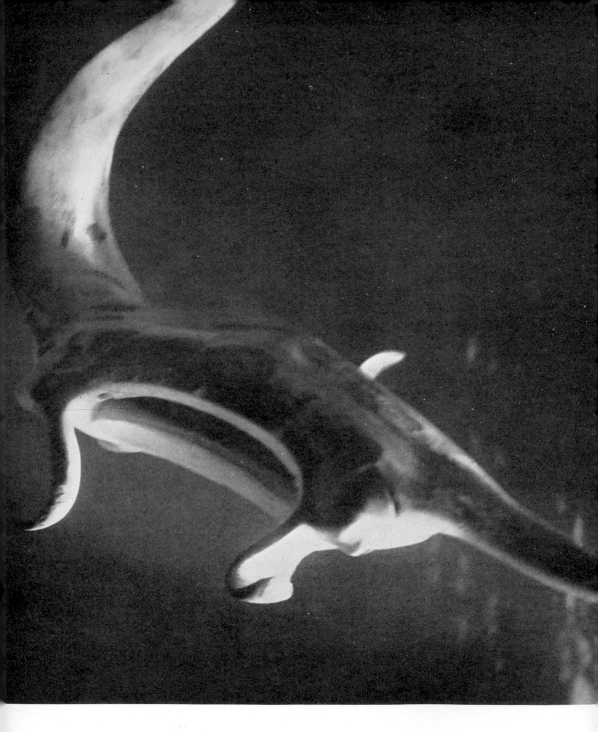

Arab fishermen call this type of horned manta a 'sea devil'; but despite its frightening appearance it eats only plankton and small fish.

A captured manta is brought to the surface (right) and hauled aboard the *Formica* (below).

A nine foot brown shark—the first shark of a dangerous species to be caught by an underwater diver with normal equipment.

The hunters set out.

The largest shark caught by the expedition.

Above: a giant cernia accompanied by pilot fish. Below: a cernia, killed in five stabs by Bucher, Vailati and Zecca, being hoisted on board.

These three pictures show a sperm whale surfacing while hunting for small tuna. The seagulls circling round it are also after the same prey—seizing the small fish that escape the whale.

This sketch shows how underwater photographs were taken with the aid of artificial light at a very considerable depth. Two men hold lighting units each of which is fitted with four 1,000-watt bulbs and connected to an electric generating set in the boat.

to study for the first time some aspects of the social or collective life of fishes, as they wanted to compare the actions of fishes in groups with their actions alone. Working at the edge of the high seas had also brought them many new specimens of the migratory fish and of molluscs, coelenterates, and plankton.

We had all learned a good deal about diving under new conditions, bringing us to the conclusion that, at present, underwater man can work no deeper than 200 to 225 feet with safety. And there are variations in this limit, depending upon the location of the work. Areas near coasts or archipelagos, where the sea bottom declines more or less gradually toward the great depths, are generally safer than the waters near islands and shoals planted in the middle of the high seas—chiefly because the marine life of the high seas is more dangerous.

Both areas, however, are safe for steady work. High-seas work needs more careful preparation and more constant attention, that's all. Currents can be incredibly strong, tiring men quickly and sometimes preventing them from coming or going as they wish. The high seas are also much more likely to suffer from bad storms that disturb work or make it difficult and dangerous.

All this, however, is no different from the situation on land. Working conditions are quite different in different parts of the world—in the tropics, in the cold north, at high altitudes, on the desert. Men know how to adapt themselves to such variations.

The extreme depths in the open sea are best suited for planned fishing, or marine 'animal-husbandry', for such places contain many more fish, and these are continually replenished by large schools of migratory fish. Also, the high seas will be the location for generators of electric power because of the terribly strong currents there.

As for our studies of the shark, we were learning that the

I

creatures of the high seas were quite different from those of the coastal regions: they were more courageous and more aggressive. But it seemed to us that the underwater man could feel sure of his superiority and security even here, provided he always kept on the alert and maintained his self-confidence.

11

Giants of the Sea

We sailed even farther south into the open sea, to the island of Gurum Shash, where the natives specialise in fishing for sharks. We wanted to see and film them at work, and we looked forward to diving near the nets dropped from their sampans. There we expected to see a good many big sharks of different varieties.

Bucher could hardly wait for the chance to hunt even larger fish, but he looked worriedly at the horizon, where he saw the first signs of the coming *khamsin*, a storm of great violence that regularly sweeps down from Egypt carrying clouds of sand and desert dust.

The storm struck before we reached the island, bringing a great grey wall that blotted out the sun. The sea changed colour, and choppy waves made the *Formica* dance and roll. Then the wind seemed to pick our ship up in its arms and whisk us over the last ten miles to the island of the sharks.

The first evening spent at Gurum Shash revealed the methods of native fishermen. Just before dusk, dozens of boats went out from the island with huge nets that were stretched out over wide areas of the sea. The ends of the nets were held up by inflated goatskins, and the sea was dotted with these bobbing figures, stomachs up and paws floating on the water as if a sudden pestilence had swept down on a strange herd.

At dawn the fishermen went out in the boats and drew in the nets, which were usually filled with sharks of all kinds, most of them dead. On board the boats, the big fish were cut open with special shark knives, and skilled hands reached in to extract the liver—the chief source of profit. On the piers, hundreds of kegs were filled with livers, sealed, and sent to Massaua, from which they were shipped to pharmaceutical firms that extracted vitamins of great value.

The other parts of the shark were thrown on the beach, covered with salt, and allowed to dry. The fins were ground into a fine dust, which became a stimulant much in demand in some Oriental countries. Enormous heads lay scattered along the beach: the long heads of the blue shark, massive heads of tiger sharks, ugly heads of the hammerheads, and the incredible heads of sawfish. The head of the sawfish, incidentally, which is about a third of the length of its body, is not used as a weapon but for a far more prosaic purpose. It is a kind of shovel, for this fish feeds on small animals and fish that are found in mud and seaweed at great depths.

Had it not been for the *khamsin* we might have encountered the swordfish near Gurum Shash, but the storm kept blowing and made the waters so muddy that immersions would not have been very fruitful. So the underwater part of our programme was abandoned, and we had to content ourselves with our documentation of the work of the natives.

Since our days in the Red Sea were numbered, we could not wait indefinitely for clear water. We pulled up anchor and headed north on our return voyage, with nothing to do but sit on deck and gaze at the horizon.

Legions and legions of sea gulls were flying overhead.

'They are following sardines,' someone said.

'Sardines?' Cecco asked. 'Since when have sardines had fins ten feet long?'

'What fins?'

'Just look out there and you will see.'

Bucher jumped up. A fin of that size meant an enormous

fish. We all started guessing at once, brought out of our lethargy in a hurry. Could they be sperm whales? Although we were sceptical, we decided to veer from our course and have a look.

When the *Formica* approached fairly near to the cloud of sea gulls, we took to the small boats and set out. We saw the birds following the big fish, watching its shadow as it disappeared beneath the surface. At that moment they plunged to the surface of the water, covering it with myriad white specks.

As we arrived among them we looked around apprehensively, wondering where and when the beast would emerge again. And we wondered how the sea gulls, resting on the water, knew in advance about the surfacing of the fish.

Suddenly there was a great clamour from the birds as they took to the air. They stretched out their necks and headed for a certain spot on the water ahead. We were right behind them when we saw, about a hundred yards ahead, a turbulence in the water and a sudden swelling of the sea. A huge black body showed itself a few feet above the surface, a body fifty-five to sixty-five feet long. A fin stuck up, straight as a sword, black as ebony.

Then we understood why the sea gulls knew where the whale was. Vast schools of little tuna raced along ahead of the whale in terror. They were only about eighteen inches long, with blue stripes and enormous eyes, and they threw themselves out of the water in an effort to escape the whale. The big beast, driven by his gargantuan hunger, was gulping down dozens and dozens of the tuna. The sea gulls noticed when the little fish leaped for their lives, showering the surface of the sea, and flew to the spot, snatching up many of those which had escaped the cavernous mouth. The tuna thought there was only one danger: the whale. They leapt in the air to escape, only to land in the beaks of the sea gulls and the claws of the sea hawks.

After watching this performance several times, as we followed along behind, we were sure that we had indeed encountered the famous sperm whale. And in a short while, we realised that there were more than one, that we had landed in the middle of an area in which they had encircled their prey, the tuna.

Masino, Giorgio, and I managed to bring our boat close to the spot where the whale emerged and learned that he came out of the water almost on his side, showing his belly. The head was square, at the bottom of which gaped a wide, cracked-lip mouth. The stomach was whitish with black lines, the ends of which looked a little red.

Under the water the whale appeared as a dark, obscure shadow. Masino watched it and speeded up the outboard motor so that we could come as close as possible for the next surfacing.

'Faster! Faster!' I shouted.

'We're going at top speed now,' Masino yelled back. 'Where is it heading?'

'To the right!' Giorgio, who was in the bow, called back. He was standing up, with a Rolleiflex in his right hand, signalling directions with his left. Masino stood up to see better, trying to manipulate the outboard motor with his legs, but the experiment brought a shower bath to us all, and he had to sit down.

'It's there!' I shouted. 'Just a bit ahead.'

'No, over to the left,' Giorgio yelled. 'Turn to the left.'

'Here it is!' I cried as the head of the whale emerged right in front of our little boat, which chugged along through spray, foam, and hundreds of sea gulls. We wanted to be near—but not that near!

Giorgio forgot all about taking pictures and grabbed on with both hands. Masino sent the boat into a wide turn to avoid hitting the whale. If he had made a sharp turn at the speed we were going, we would all have been in the water.

We kept going, keeping our eyes skinned. Some sea gulls, we noticed, preferred to stay on the water, a little to one side, instead of plunging down for the little tuna. They waited until the spouting of the whale hurled up dozens of fish and scattered them over a wide area.

The contest between the whale, the sea gulls, and the tuna lasted more than two hours. Suddenly we saw that the sun was going down, and the wind coming up. Looking northward, we observed the giant grey curtain of the *khamsin* heading in our direction. Within a few minutes it struck the sea and us with a steady, violent blow.

There was not a moment to lose. The boats left whale, tuna, and sea gulls to run fast for the *Formica*, which was busy blowing its siren to warn us of the approaching peril. The race between us and the heart of the *khamsin* was won by a breath. The boats were not even hoisted aboard when the first bad squalls hit us.

As we continued on our way north through the storm, there was lively discussion about our unexpected meeting with the whales, mingled with regrets that we had been unable to photograph them. We had no idea that the sea held in store for us an experience that would wipe out all regrets quickly.

It happened as we were getting near Massaua. We stopped at the madreporic barrier of Dur-Gaam, a little island at the tip of the Dahlak Archipelago, to take on supplies of fish for exchange in the big port. While there, we put in a little time fishing and filming.

As we worked, we all felt that there was something strange in the air—or rather, in the sea. Unusual noises occasionally reached our ears: eerie whistles, shrieks, and cries that were completely inexplicable. They made us interrupt our work and look at each other questioningly.

We began to guess about the origin of the noises. Some thought that they had some trouble with their eardrums; others suggested that somewhere about there was a lost respirator. Then our imaginings became wilder—as absurd as the noises that we heard without quite believing that we heard them.

But we went on working just the same. About four-thirty that afternoon we returned to the *Formica*, tired and hungry as usual. Some went to take a shower, some headed for the mineral water, some started arranging the specimens they had collected, and some went to the galley to goad Peppe the cook into hurrying the meal. The crew raised the anchor, and we left Dur-Gaam for Massaua.

Half an hour later one of the sailors on deck began to shout like a madman.

'Dolphins! Lots of them! Hundreds of them!'

We rushed to the rail to find that the *Formica* was literally surrounded by an enormous school of big fish that jumped and shot about in every direction.

But they were not dolphins. Their snouts did not end like beaks, the colour was not greenish yellow, and—most important —these beasts were at least four times as big as dolphins. The heads were enormous, round and blunt, without projection of any kind. No, these were not dolphins, but they were certainly Globicephala.

The Globicephala are cetaceans, brother beasts of the whales and dolphins. Like most cetaceans, they live in great schools travelling together. The *Formica* was surrounded by such a school, with these big fish tirelessly circling round it.

Here was the chance to make up for our lost time farther south. It was probably the first chance underwater men had ever had to dive among fish of this size. Imperturbably the creatures continued their minuet round the *Formica*, with an almost rhythmic splash of water as they submerged, interrupted by the sonorous sound of their breathing as they came to the surface.

Three of us prepared for the exciting dive. The crew were terrified and looked at us as if they would never see us again. The captain tried to dissuade us, and so did Benedetto, but we were too busy to listen.

'Are you ready?' Bruno shouted from the rail, already prepared to jump.

'Just a moment,' Giorgio implored, tightening the last screws on the case of the underwater camera so fast that he seemed to be a juggler.

Bruno, Giorgio, and I were about to leap from the side of the boat when Cecco appeared, leaping across the deck.

'Just a moment, boys, just a moment. Be calm. You say they are Globicephala, probably blackfish, but you can't be sure from here.'

'Well then,' Bruno said, 'we'll go into the water to find out.'

'Wait a moment,' Cecco argued. 'They might be Orca— killer whales. Those are creatures that don't fool round. They attack and devour in a few minutes. Now, I don't *think* they are killer whales, but let's be sure. Killer whales and blackfish are quite similar.'

'We shall be careful,' Bruno said. 'We'll stay close to each other and not go far from the ship.'

'Come on, or it will be too late to take pictures,' I said.

'Are you really going?' Cecco asked.

'Yes, right now,' Bruno said.

'Then I'll go with you.'

Cecco darted into the cabin to put on mask and fins. But he had nothing else to carry. It would have been silly to think of weapons against such beasts.

With a splash we leaped into the sea, which at this point was at least a thousand feet deep. We could not see the coasts, and so found ourselves suspended in a world of dark blue and impenetrable black, blue around us, black beneath. The setting sun sent its yellow streaks to pierce the obscurity, but its rays died after a few yards in the water.

Under the water we could hear, loudly and plainly, the sounds that we had been hearing faintly all day. Whistles and shrieks echoed from one part of the sea to another, sounding near at times, then farther away, reverberating and crisscrossing. Their first effect was to terrify us, accustomed as we were to complete silence in the depths.

It is hard to describe the sounds in words. I think 'shriek' comes closest, but it is really a cross between a shriek and a whistle.

We tried to trace the sounds to their origin and finally realised that they came from spots that showed long silvery lines of bubbles extending to the surface. We followed the bubbles and there, about eighty feet below us, we saw enormous shadows. Moving very slowly, the big creatures seemed to be rising gradually. We could see them more clearly—clear enough to be sure of what they were. They were not killer whales. Cecco signalled that they were definitely Globicephala, blackfish—sometimes called pilot whales. We decided to go and meet them.

We dived down, finning rapidly, and after a few seconds came close to some of the big blackfish. They had immense tapering bodies, stocky and almost round, with huge horizontal tails. Each one of us selected a fish and swam as close to it as possible. I came within about thirty-five feet of a huge creature and saw that two smaller ones followed along under it: baby blackfish about thirteen or fourteen feet long. The children of this mammal are not weaned for a long time after their birth, but follow their mothers constantly—very different from other marine creatures, whose children are on their own almost from the moment of birth.

Some of the big fish swam near us and turned to look. They did not like to have us behind them, and when they realised that we were in that position they moved brusquely and turned. I thought the end of the world was coming. A huge mass of water moved, whirled, and turned. My movements had no effect against it, and I felt myself dragged, turned over twice, and sucked several yards below. But nothing else happened. The blackfish had just created a tremendous current of water by the movement of their tails when they decided to turn. They disappeared from our view.

We sped toward the surface, while the shrieks of the black-fish spread and dissolved gradually in the distance. For the first time we had heard the language of fish when they were disturbed. We knew that fish could speak, or communicate, but their sounds are generally beyond the range of our hearing, just as ultra-violet and infra-red light are beyond the range of our sight.

When we came to the surface of the water, we swam together and started shouting to each other at once, comparing our impressions of the magnificent sight we had just seen.

The shouts of those on board the *Formica* brought us back to our senses.

'They're turning! They're turning!'

We looked round and saw the big blackfish advancing toward us. We could not believe our eyes, for the picture before us looked so much like some illustration out of a book of myths—like the one of Venus being drawn in a sea shell over the water by four leaping dolphins.

Eight blackfish in perfect formation came directly toward the four of us in the water. About every hundred and fifty feet they leaped from the water in graceful, dripping curves, with sprays of water shooting toward the sky. As they plunged under again, eight tails in line waved a moment before disappearing.

The big tapering bodies continued to advance as in a naval manœuvre. When they came near, we all dived as deep as possible and looked up. Suddenly we saw them; they seemed to be plunging down from the sky above. The water was agitated as if by an earthquake, and their shrieks became louder and louder, until they seemed about to break our eardrums.

They saw us, dived straight down past us, and continued moving toward the depths. In a few seconds they were quite deep, but before they disappeared in the blackness they all rolled over on their sides and looked back at us with their big white eyes, curious but neither frightened nor contemptuous. And then they were gone.

Before the echoes of their shrieks had faded, another adventure was upon us. A fish appeared, very small in comparison with those we had just seen—but it was a shark. It was a kind we had never seen before, moving at great speed and quite rigid, without the usual sinuous motion. Then we saw that it was a white shark—the shark for whom the word 'man-eater' was created.

The voices of the blackfish disappeared, and we returned to the silence we were accustomed to in the depths. Circling, the white shark approached us without haste. We surfaced slowly, not wanting it to think that we were afraid of it. The moment our heads came out of the water I yelled as loudly as I could, 'Masino, a launch!'

The others kept an eye on the shark. We could not move towards the small boat that was quickly lowered because we did not want to give the impression of fleeing. Someone had to come from the *Formica* and pull us out of the water. The best thing for us to do at the moment was to remain motionless, back to back, keeping our eyes on the circling shark that came closer and closer.

Were we afraid? Well, I was certainly afraid, and I think my friends were, too. It was the first time that a shark seriously frightened me. Its sly advance, majestic and sinister, in a bottomless sea, and in growing darkness—yes, it was frightening. The circumstances were all in the shark's favour: a proven man-eater, on the high seas, we on the surface, men without weapons of any kind, and darkness.

The seconds seemed like hours as the boat advanced from the *Formica*. It was hard not to leap aboard, for the shark was coming close. If we had tried to leap, the shark probably would have chosen that moment of fear and flight to attack.

They pulled us quickly into the little boat, and in a few minutes we were back on the *Formica*. The sun was disappearing, and the Red Sea deserved its name. Far away we saw the blackfish, leaping from the water.

Our finest adventure in the Blue Continent had ended.

The King is Dead

Look at those reefs, those broken black points that appear and disappear in the waves of the sea.

Here a sampan full of pilgrims on the way to Mecca lost their lives one night many years ago. A screaming mass of people fell into the sea, and one good man drowned. Some managed to stay afloat by holding to pieces of wood. Others tried to swim to shore. Suddenly the water began to boil and the air filled with frightened cries.

Sharks!

After five terrible minutes, the sea was calm again. An enormous stain of blood spread across the surface, which survivors could smell in the darkness. The fish completed their man-eating quickly and then disappeared. Out of forty-seven people, only seven survived. The tragedy was complete.

Now close your eyes an instant. The scene shifts from night to day, to a morning in May last year.

Around these same reefs are some boats, and if you look closely you will recognise us. There is Masino preparing his Aquaflex to the accompaniment of a few oaths. Bucher is loading his gun. Bruno is talking to me about the subject of to-day's filming, and Enza is slipping on her fins. Here we are, twelve people who spend from five to six hours a day under water. We have all seen sharks, but not one of us has even been scratched by them. Possibly a little frightened from time to time when a shark passes too close for comfort, but nothing serious. Yet we dive in the exact spot where dozens of human bodies were devoured by a school of sharks in one terrible moment—perhaps among the very same sharks.

Why does the shark treat the poor Moslem travelling to Mecca differently from the way he treats us?

The shark is accustomed to feed on wounded fish, on carcasses. He seems to know that the bobbing lump of a drowned corpse is a succulent mouthful and that there is no risk involved for him. He circles round under it to take aim, then attacks. He makes no distinction between a drowned or shipwrecked Moslem and someone swimming on the surface. They look the same to him. Once he attacks, draws blood, and is not attacked in return, he closes in for the kill.

We have photographed the shark swimming peacefully among schools of scad, his favourite food. He attacks only if one of them is wounded or in difficulty. To him, underwater man is just another living fish, of a different species—to be examined carefully. But it is enough to make a dive or violent gesture in his direction for him to turn tail and run.

If someone asks whether or not sharks attack men, the answer must be another question: what shark, what man, in what circumstances? After five months of voluntary co-existence with the King of the Sea, we have found ourselves in complete disagreement with the widespread 'bloody mythology' of sharks.

I would not advise anyone to take a swim across the six hundred yards of the channel at Great Dahlak without a mask. On the other hand, I would take along anyone who wanted to come right to the bottom with an auto-respirator, where a bomb has exploded and where twenty or thirty sharks, from seven to fourteen feet long, are darting about.

After taking the proper precautions and making the necessary preparations, one may safely descend to the depths, as our experiences prove. But one must consider that a substantial difference exists between 'coastal sharks' and 'sharks of the high seas'. The sharks encountered on our trip outside the Dahlak were less timid than those we saw at first. The shark which assailed the swordfish and was then shot by Bruno as we came from Suez to Massaua, behaved more violently than any other we met along the coast. The white shark that circled round us after our encounter with the blackfish was probably violent. Although it didn't attack, very likely it was just waiting for the right moment. Certainly its behaviour was not reassuring. So there are sharks and sharks, just as there are men and men. The shark is essentially a fish of the high seas. His cowardice prompts him to assault other beings only when they are in a disadvantageous position. Only at night does the shark go hunting. Then he knows he can attack suddenly and without being seen.

It seemed to us that sharks found in the narrow coastal strip where frogmen work most of the time were absolutely harmless. Those found in the high seas present a potential peril, for they are in or near the natural habitat of anthropophagous fish. But even here, having taken proper precautions, underwater man can always rely on his psychological superiority to feel relatively secure. At night, in the open ocean, the picture changes. Here the shark is truly the King of the Sea, not to be challenged with impunity by amphibious man.

Certain behaviour patterns of the shark have been a controversial question for some time. What makes the shark arrive a few seconds after we have shot a fish? Obviously neither sight nor smell. To us the only possible explanation is acoustics. Sharks must hear the scream of the wounded fish. Or perhaps they are attracted by the fish's violent movements. If you throw a dead fish in the water, even if it is still bleeding, it brings no sharks. But throw in a half-dead fish, not bleeding at all, and the sharks come at full speed. All of us were gradually convinced that they respond to some sound or vibration emitted by the fish in peril. An adventure of Cecco's helped to confirm us in this belief.

Once he was submerged about fifty feet down, looking toward the bottom, his gun pointed below. He felt something bearing down on him. Raising his eyes, he saw six large tuna, about fifty pounds each, quickly marching against him.

Instinctively, almost as if parrying a blow, Cecco raised the barrel of his gun. The sharpness of his movement frightened the six fish. They all jumped and reversed their route. The reaction was as sudden as if one of the fish had been hit.

A second later, the tuna had disappeared, but three sharks circled round Cecco with the resentful air of a maid summoned by the bell by mistake. Why?

They arrived like lightning because they had evidently 'heard' or 'felt' something: the cry of fear emitted by the six tuna, or the sharp vibrations sent out as they twisted to avoid Cecco's gun. They ran because of a sonorous call, naturally not audible to our ears.

I would say that sharks possess a complex character. They are very stupid and incredibly cowardly. Just as we indulgently excuse certain of our acquaintances with the phrase, 'He was dropped on his head as a baby,' when we do not want to consider them responsible for their stupidities, so we can excuse sharks because they belong to the prehistoric Selachii family. These are animals without skeletons or spinal columns, with the smallest of brains that rests in a cranium made of cartilage.

From their stupidity comes their cowardice, because obviously they do not believe in their own power. They do not appreciate the psychology of other beings that live around them and they do not realise that no one would be able to withstand their attack.

Probably the best way to explain the way we came to feel about sharks is to tell of the argument which took place between Enza Bucher and Raimondo.

One day a bomb had been dropped and there were dead fish and sharks of every size and type round the boat. Raimondo,

135

K

in the middle of his complicated job of loading his 'supergun', was not yet ready to go into action. Enza was ready and eager to jump in the water. The couple argued violently, and as I listened to them from a distance I could not help sympathising with what I took to be Raimondo's concern for his wife. But as I came nearer I realised that the argument had arisen for quite a different reason.

Raimondo was pounding the ship's rail. 'Once and for all, Enza,' he shouted, 'don't dive! Don't dive! If you do, you'll frighten all the sharks away!'

By exploding some of the myths which surround sharks, I do not mean to detract from the courage shown by other under-water expeditions. The amount of courage necessary to undertake the risks of shark hunting can be clearly shown by comparing big-game hunting on land to big-game hunting under-water. The beasts of the forest—lion, tiger, elephant, rhinoceros—are met face to face on equal ground and with a gun that has perhaps a range of six hundred yards. We face the beasts of the sea, on the contrary, in an element to which we are not accustomed, and we have a gun that delivers a single blow with a range of eight or nine feet. Land beasts can be seen several hundred yards away, while underwater visibility is at most thirty-three yards, often only ten or twelve feet. These are distances that a shark travelling at forty miles an hour—or more—can cover in a fraction of a second. With this in mind, you can easily understand that big-game hunting under water was the most remarkable feat of our expedition.

In their incessant circling, sharks have parasites of two types as inseparable companions, the pilot fish and the remora, which in exchange for bits of their patron's food perform operations of cleaning or according to recent theories guiding.

The pilot fish, a little fellow with black and yellow stripes, owes its name to the fact that we see it always a few inches ahead of the shark's snout. 'The shark is very myopic,' one authority has claimed, 'and the small fish that precede it act as its guide.' However, it was difficult to imagine such small fish being able to reach the high speed at which the shark moves. Then, too, the sight of the shark is just about as good as that of other fish—so that although the name of the pilot fish remains, it no longer has any significance.

It seems probable that the small fish travels ahead of the shark effortlessly, pushed along by the great quantity of water displaced by the big creature in much the same way as a surf board rides the crest of a wave.

The remora is longer than the pilot fish, and follows the shark by clinging to his belly or fins by means of a sort of suction disc that opens on the parasite's head.

One day while Silverio was hunting down below, a pilot fish passed in front of his mask, wiggling its tail a few inches from Silverio's nose. He did not disturb it but allowed it to continue its nibbling. No matter where he turned, the pilot fish stayed there in front of his mask. He surfaced, calling to us to observe the strange phenomenon. When he went down the pilot fish took up its position once more. Annoyed, Silverio tried to get rid of it, but in vain. Nothing would induce the small fish to leave, not even Silverio's menacing gestures. I followed, waiting patiently for it to make advances to me, when Silverio finally went up above. But although the pilot fish realised its loss and seemed quite upset that its strange new 'fish' had gone out of the water and left it in the lurch, it did not adopt me.

Something of this sort occurred some time later to Masino. Bruno shot a shark. After a brief struggle the shark was dead. Masino dashed to the scene with his Aquaflex and noticed that while the wounded shark made its last thrusts and was being carried to the surface, a remora, that had been attached underneath it, detached itself and darted around frantically. Finally, bewildered without a home, it made for Masino like a ball of fire.

Masino took his eye away from the view finder and looked around. Where was the remora? It was hanging beneath the roundish belly of the movie camera, mistaking it for the belly of a shark!

These stories are more proof that we underwater men are considered to be fish, by other fish. This fact explains much of their behaviour towards us.

One day at Dur-Gaam, a shark advanced towards Gianni and me when we were on the bottom with respirators. It displayed a mixture of cowardice and curiosity as it circled warily about us. Evidently we were something troublesome, new, unknown, to its eyes. It wanted to look, but at the same time it was mortally afraid.

The remora, hanging by its left fin, suddenly detached itself from the shark and made a quick reconnaissance. The shark was still circling round fearfully, like a man moving in the dark expecting an ambush. The remora, ending its tour, returned to attach itself to the shark. At the unexpected touch, the shark gave a violent start, like a man in the dark frightened by a sudden noise. There was a flash, a leap, and quick flight.

It was excellent news for our programme when we found the sharks afraid of us, for this gave us the confidence to get as close to them as possible to film them. The greatest difficulty, in fact, was not the ferocity of these beasts, but the problem of getting near them without making them flee in terror. Even more difficult was the task of getting a man and a shark in the same picture, particularly when the water was turbid.

The best system was not to work in two-man teams, but to have another helper behind one to shoot at a threatening fish.

Another notable difficulty was that of colour, for the sharks look so similar to the dark bottom of the sea over which they move. It was not the tuna or the shiny scad that were hard to shoot seventy-five or a hundred feet down, but the metallic-grey sharks. Photographs with the flash turned out rather well, for the beast became illuminated with strange reflections which were quite effective. But with movies there was a great problem. We solved it by shooting the sharks from a little above in order to see them against the white sand, by taking them with rocks or madrepore behind, by taking them from the bottom looking up, against the light.

From the strictly photographic point of view, another problem was the speed of the sharks. Our photos were generally made at 1/50 of a second, but even so some turned out blurred. Giorgio's flash was a great aid. If the subject was near, with its help one was able always to keep the largest opening of the lens and use the fastest speed. The lightning flash of a shark swallowing a fish, the most striking black and white photograph we took, was taken at a yard's distance, 3.5 lens opening, and at a speed of 1/1000 of a second. As actors, sharks are rather difficult to handle, but they are exceptionally photogenic and the results are worth all the trouble.

But even though the shark is not the phenomenon of courage we once thought him, he is still a stupendous adversary to encounter.

In short, despite its six rows of teeth, each an inch long, its six hundred pounds, and thirteen feet of length, the shark, ninety-nine times out of a hundred, will turn tail and flee if one so much as says 'Boo!' to his face. Nevertheless whenever one meets it, one feels one's heart beat a little faster. It is still the King of the Sea, and monarchs have a special fascination, for the eyes of even the most rabid republican, even after they have been deposed.

13

Bucher's Triumph

THE day finally came when we returned to Massaua after our last spell of work in the Dahlak. We were ready to go home. During the return voyage we would draw our final conclusions, draft the reports on the three programmes we had undertaken and outline the potentialities of the Blue Continent. In the main, we felt satisfied with the results we had obtained.

'Personally I am not satisfied at all,' said Bucher, as the *Formica* noisily rounded the breakwater and entered the port of Massaua in the last light of evening.

According to our champion, there was something missing. He felt that he had not found the crowning link that would complete the chain of victories of the sports group. For the past month he had stubbornly searched for the right dramatic climax, for something at the end of the expedition to equal his remarkable breaking of the world's record at its beginning. Sometimes, in this desperate search for a special victory that would cast all others in the shade, he had returned to the water at twilight, when working in the Blue Continent became dangerous. Almost anything might have happened—one of those sharks coming up unseen from the deep sea, a giant manta amusing itself on the surface in the rippling waves. He sought out danger in an effort to reach the pinnacle he dreamed of.

No one else was dissatisfied. We tried to persuade Bucher that he had performed miraculous feats on the expedition, but he brushed us aside. He was not worried about the good opinion of others. He had not reached the goal he set for himself. He wanted a really great capture, a victory over the biggest or strongest or most dangerous fish in the world that would emphatically confirm the superiority of man over all other animals in the depths of the sea.

Bucher could think of nothing else. And we began to feel that if fortune did not favour him during our return voyage, he would be deeply disappointed in spite of the important objectives already reached. There was not much time left. The expedition was fast drawing to an end.

'We have to solder the zinc cases.'

'Have you got the film ready to send?'

'Get busy with those little tanks of air.'

'Vailati, have you found out about the fuel?'

Directions, orders, and recommendations crisscrossed as we docked. Then we scattered on shore, to work or amuse ourselves until morning. Night fell, and with it interminable hours of suffocating heat. The immoderately heavy humidity of this region bathes everything as if the rains had fallen. At last daybreak came to the *Formica*, and the sun gradually dried off everything. Its rays began to strike the houses, cranes, ships, the waters of the harbour. People began to move about the streets of the town; a few boats set out into the bay.

We were all up early, for we had many tasks to get through before our departure. We were on shore finishing these chores, but no one noticed that Raimondo and Enza were missing. They had risen very early, before anyone else. . . .

Suddenly we saw people running from every direction— Italians and natives, running toward the harbour. The drowsy morning calm of Massaua vanished all at once. People were shouting excitedly. We followed the shouts, running with the others.

'To the harbour, to the harbour! Bucher has caught a devilfish!'

'Your Bucher has taken an enormous manta! Run!'

The white rowboat of the sports group was being moored near the *Formica*, which was crowded with people jumping from the pier to the ship and back again, all trying to get a better view.

In the rowboat sat Bucher and his wife, radiantly happy, with a native at the oars. One look and we knew that Bucher had found the missing link, and accomplished the crowning achievement he longed for.

Something was slung across the prow of the boat, something whitish, and disproportionately large. The most vital part of this large beast had a harpoon planted in its centre, and it was giving the last feeble beats of its wings and tail.

It was a giant manta—the prize Bucher had wanted. It weighed over 330 pounds, the largest we had ever caught, and provided a brilliant finale to the adventures of the National Underwater Expedition in the Red Sea. The devil of the sea had had its wings clipped.

Raimondo finally came on board the *Formica*, and, after the big excitement had died down and the crowds thinned out, we were able to hear his story.

The drama had taken place in the port of Massaua. This was a pool of deep muddy water noted for its dramatic stories of sharks. It was a totally different scene from all others of underwater hunting. There was none of the solitude, the silence, the grandeur of the usual hunt on the shoals or among the reefs. Instead there was a city in the background, ships being loaded by cranes and natives going to work on the quays.

The spectacle took place practically in the centre of a stadium, with hundreds of eyewitnesses, and a cheering audience, like a sensational bullfight.

Bucher had not slept well, as a result of thinking about the final prize he coveted. He and his wife had arisen before dawn, gone down to the harbour and found the boat and an oarsman. A light breeze blew across the water, sending long waves in the direction of the wind.

As the first light of the sun struck the harbour, Bucher saw two equidistant fins, cutting the surface in a leisurely fashion. Then, between them, there was a third fin. The two fins were the points of wings beating against the sea. The third was the little dorsal fin. It was a manta!

The distance between the two parallel fins not only told Bucher the identity of the creature but its size—it was almost ten feet across! He knew that he was dealing with a huge specimen, so he did not lose a second. As the boat drew near, he threw himself into the water with only a face mask and spring gun, while his wife tried to guide him toward the spot where the manta had appeared on the surface.

Suddenly someone on shore spotted the manta and the hunter pursuing it. He called to others, and in a short time the shore was dotted with people who shouted like madmen, like fans of a great 'star' at a sports event. They cheered for the little man who swam steadily and with great courage to track down and capture singlehanded a beast three times as large as he. Soon there were people on the piers, on the rooftops, and even climbing up on top of the cranes.

They saw Raimondo approach the manta, dive, and aim. They held their breath, but the hunter emerged without having shot. He had not found the right spot, or the right distance.

Man and manta went through more circular manœuvres, on the bottom, and near the surface. The manta made wide sweeping turns, moved this way and that to escape. Sometimes it looked as if Bucher was near enough to shoot, but he knew to the inch the effective range of his gun, and the strength of its blow. And he wanted to kill the beast with one perfect shot.

Bucher did not allow himself to be overcome by temptation. He didn't rush or hurry. Finally, he succeeded in placing himself above the path of the manta, in a perfect position for a magnificent shot. The beast advanced, and saw Raimondo above him when he was only a few yards away. It dived for the bottom, but at that moment Bucher dived too and fired his gun. Not content with the great force behind the springs of his gun, he hurled another harpoon with a vigorous swing of his arm.

Both harpoons struck hard, in exactly the right spot.

The manta made a start, jerked, and increased its speed. Raimondo was dragged for some distance, and then the sounding line joining harpoon to gun snapped. But there was still the line from the harpoon to the large float. This in turn bounced across the surface of the waves, as if propelled by an invisible motor, as the manta dragged it along in its frantic attempt to escape.

The audience, realising that the beast had been hit, screamed and applauded. They sent up resounding cheers for Raimondo as he finned like a madman behind the racing float, hoping to give the manta a third and final blow.

Bucher was afraid that the beast would be able to break the sounding line, particularly when he saw it trying to drag the float to the bottom. The taut line jerked so violently that the float, despite its size and weight, was under the water half of the time in its dash round the harbour.

Finally, the manta found a little open spot of sand on the bottom and crouched, with the spear in the centre of its head. Bucher arrived at full speed, dived, and prepared to give the final blow. But the manta, although almost exhausted, saw his implacable enemy above and beat its pointed wings frantically, using its last drop of energy in an effort to reach the open sea. But he could not go far. The harpoon had worked into the gills, and blood spurted out, a long, dense, brown strip like the thread of a tangled skein, draining the manta of all its strength.

The two terrorised eyes at the base of the horns were already glazed when Bucher, seeing the beast suddenly stop and drop to the bottom, knew that the battle was won. The whole fight had taken him nearly ninety minutes. He fell upon his prey and brought it to the surface. As far as we knew underwater man had for the first time won the battle against the giant manta ray in its own habitat, with the technique, weapons, and equipment of the underwater hunter.

A big crowd gathered about the prize as if it were holding a meeting. From the stern of the *Formica* the trophy was transferred to a jeep. The crowd parted to let the jeep pass. Then the inevitable photo. The manta was to be presented to the fish-meal factory. As it travelled across Massaua, our hosts witnessed the glorious end of the sports programme of the Italian Expedition.

14

Return to Land and Air

ONE morning the *Formica* gave a much longer blow of its siren than usual. It bade good-bye to Massaua, to the sea, to Dahlak, to friends, both native and Italian, waving from the quay. We departed for the north, and for Italy.

But we had decided against a direct trip through the Red Sea. Cecco and I had persuaded Bruno to stop at least a couple of times for forty-eight hours at interesting points in the northern waters. The first stop would be at the coral barrier of Mersa Halaib, in the Sudan.

Four days of droning and light rolling as we plodded slowly mile after mile through the water. One day the sea was calm, and I threw a harpoon into a stupendous dolphin. It appeared at the prow with six or seven companions, making agile leaps from the water, slipping quickly under the keel and shooting out on the other side like lightning. It was the largest of the group and the largest I had ever seen.

Five months before, we had harpooned a dolphin shortly after leaving Crete, after which a terrible storm had struck us. When my dolphin was hoisted aboard on this return voyage, it lay on its side 'crying' a long time before it died. Subdued moans came from its opening and closing mouth, causing the crew to mutter and predict a terrible storm.

'You will see,' they said. 'When dolphins cry, they call the wind.'

We smiled then. But that night a storm hit us, and we almost wound up in the mouths of fishes.

The next day, standing on the prow with my harpoon in hand, my arm raised for a blow at another leaping dolphin, I felt the glare of the captain and heard his warning. I waited for a fraction of a second. If I should hit the dolphin, the captain would certainly be in a bad humour. Perhaps we would have bad weather again, another storm.

I finally decided to chance it! I threw!

'Beautiful! Caught! Caught!' Cecco yelled, seeing my mighty thrust of the harpoon into the body of the dolphin as it slipped from the side of the ship.

'Caught! Caught!' I shouted, running along the rail.

'Stop! Stop the engines!' screamed Giorgio. The line connecting the harpoon to a hook on the ship unwound quickly. Then a dull thud. The cable was broken, just as the *Formica* slowed down. The dolphin had escaped.

No dolphin, no storm. Peppe, Mollo, and the captain assured me that blows from the tail of the other dolphins had liberated their companion. It was still alive, so no storm would come. And none did.

Mersa Halaib is a vast gulf surrounded by a desert and mountains. The sea was ruffled by a strong wind that blew from the interior, bending the palms. A row of black huts dotted the beach between the water and the desert.

The *Formica* anchored in the centre of the bar, with a coralline barrier stretching beyond her. It was quite late, but not too late for a dive. Bruno, Giorgio, and I went in.

The sandy bottom rose steeply and suddenly, and we found ourselves above the shoal in less than two feet of water. We swam around rapidly, then the wind blew up long waves that raised us and pushed us toward the waters outside the barrier.

There we leaped into the open sea and went down to look at the barrier. It was altogether different from that at Dahlak—

in colour, in the architecture of the madrepore, in the luxuriant richness of its blossoming coral. We found a completely new type of pomacentrid, that dotted everything with little specks of yellow and red.

The next morning Giorgio and I loaded the respirators to 150 atmospheres, their maximum, to try a rather exceptional dive to the very base of the barrier. At eleven, having shot some scenes, we drew away from the others and followed the winding path of the barrier's descent. It was useless to carry the movie camera because at that depth there would not be enough light for pictures. But we took the camera with the flash. Our bathing suits bulged with flash bulbs to be exploded below.

We dived straight down—thirty, sixty, eighty feet. I felt my chest contract and my ears ache. Signalling to Giorgio to stop ten seconds, I swallowed and pushed the air from my nose into my ears. I heard inside my head a dull thud, a series of crashes, and then silence. There was no more pain. The internal passage of the ear was free. The air of the respirator equalised very well the external pressure.

Going on down, we passed a spacious terrace on which a forest of long, threadlike little sticks bobbed. They were 'coral whips', of which there are countless varieties in the marine depths. I looked toward the surface and realised that we could no longer see our sky, nor the undulating designs of the waves or any other signs of the external world. Only diffused luminescence and a few feeble rays of light—uncertain and fragile—pushed toward the bottom.

The bottom was very dark. All colours had disappeared, leaving us in a field of blue-green which became darker and darker. After about four minutes of descent we reached 175 feet, the end. We had gradually become accustomed to the disappearance of the light. We were very near the barrier, in its blue-black shadow. There was some madrepore, but it was small and illuminated

148

only on its external crown. Some fire coral offered the effect of light, and we saw some parrot fish swimming about. A few sharks appeared and disappeared.

A school of dark blue parrot fish with clear, enormous, dilated eyes advanced with tails in air, beaks grazing or nibbling along the bottom. A carangid, with its back crowned by a series of large thorns, darted toward Giorgio.

A sudden flash blinded our eyes. The fish glittered for a fraction of a second, like a mirror when it reflects the sun. Then all returned to darkness. All the fish round us had fled, frightened.

The flash signalled the start of our work at this depth. We had been there twenty seconds and would be able to remain another minute and a half. The strong pressure at this depth would empty the tanks of compressed air quickly, and we wanted to take some photos to discover if the brilliant colours of the surface existed here. The obscurity was broken by a series of flashes of great power. The colours were there.

I saw the black wall hanging over us frescoed with thousands of tints—magnificent yellows and reds and oranges. I turned to Giorgio. He saw them, too, he told me with a nod of his head. Later the developed films confirmed our impressions. One might ask why nature placed brilliant colours down there, where no one can see them, where no light penetrates. Since the beginning of the world they have been there, but they were seen as colours only in the moments when we photographed them.

Surfacing toward the increasing light gave us a very pleasant sensation, especially as the water gradually got warmer.

The *Formica* left Mersa Halaib and headed north again. Aboard, there was some excitement round Enza's cabin, for she was in bed waiting for her leg to swell up like a balloon and for a fever that might rise very high.

She had shot a large sea eel. (Have I already commented on

Enza's fixation about sea eels? At Dahlak she caught a monstrous one, weighing more than twenty-six pounds.) Skilfully she had dragged it from a grotto, jerked it along the bottom, and surfaced with it. Just as she was throwing it into the boat, the sea eel, which was twisted around the spear, loosened itself and like lightning wound itself round Enza's calf, biting her severely.

Vailati immediately grabbed it and flung it into the sea. Then he sucked and squeezed the wound, making the blood rush out freely. After half a day, except for pain, nothing happened. The expected infection had not shown its symptoms—a sign that Vailati had succeeded in forcing the poison out with the blood.

This was the only successful aggression of any so-called dangerous fish in the five months of our work—a good score. Which brings us to a consideration of the results obtained by the expedition.

What about the sports group? The first point established, it seemed to us, was that even when they are hungry, 'dangerous' fish permit underwater men to work without troubling them. Except in the one case with Enza, these fish did not even trouble men who killed and molested other fish around them.

The twenty sharks of every type captured, the great mantas harpooned by Bucher, Vailati, and Zecca, the victories over the giant cernias, over the barracudas and others—these not only represented the trophies of the hunters but showed that man could work in security in the Blue Continent for the reason that he could conquer all his enemies there.

Perhaps as important as anything else in the work of the sportsmen was their enormous contribution to the collections of the scientific group.

'Where next, Bruno?' I asked, as he bent over a nautical map.

'What do you say to this place?'

With his finger he showed me an island located nearly in the centre of the Red Sea, fifty miles farther north. It was Zabargiadh, one of the thousands of deserted islands of this sea.

'It is a fearful volcanic peak,' he said, 'that rises vertically for about 2,800 feet. We should see something beautiful there.'

At five o'clock on the morning of 18 May, the *Formica's* siren made the sleepers jump from their bunks. We had arrived at Zabargiadh. Dark rocks jutted out steeply and jaggedly, and we could see no vegetation at all.

At seven o'clock two boats headed for the shore. The sun was high on the horizon, and the sea had become a glaring green. The water was icy; when we stuck a foot in, it seemed to be bitten. We saw dark holes in the sides of the mountain—entrances to diamond mines abandoned years ago after fruitless search. Farther along, almost on the beach, we saw two small graves of stone where two Egyptian soldiers were buried who had died of hunger and thirst, having been left to watch the abandoned mines. They had been forgotten.

When I dived into the sea, I was paralysed by the icy water. I almost died. I froze up, closed my eyes, and descended while massaging myself briskly. After going down a few yards, I opened my eyes.

An unforgettable spectacle lay before me. The water was as clear as the sky in the mountains. It had none of the muddiness of Dahlak. The madreporic barrier ran for a great distance, looking like the side of a castle in a medieval legend, quite different from the others we had seen. The formations were less colourful and numerous, but the general architecture from the bottom, at a hundred feet, to the surface was absolutely new, fantastic, complicated by deep crevices, terraces, and large towers that rose up one by one from the sandy bottom. Shooting around near me were dozens of yellow fish about three feet long, with a pointed horn between the eyes. As they passed along the rocks, their groups were divided by a column of madrepore. Other new fish, or at least different varieties from those seen in the south, passed near me. Conspicuously absent were barracuda and angelfish. It is incredible how much the fauna changes in a distance of a hundred miles or so.

What about sharks? We were so used to seeing them that we didn't pay much attention even when there were five or six near by, circling us. We could see their shiny dark bodies from far off in this water that glittered like a diamond. Zabargiadh merits its name as the island of diamonds, if only because of the waters round it.

Bucher guided me to the entrance of a grotto, opening into the barrier. I advanced in complete darkness with my arms outstretched to keep me from colliding with any obstacles. This was the kind of cave in which monsters were supposed to dwell, but I found no monsters. Raimondo waited for me at the entrance while I went to the end so that I could photograph it with a flash. When I touched the rock of the end wall, I turned. About forty feet away I saw a sinuous light from the opening, an irregular streak in the centre of a black field.

A dark shadow appeared in the light. It was Raimondo, whose respirator gave out a rhythmic silver necklace of air bubbles. From clefts above descended a few fine violet light-rays which became luminous in the blackness. The sight, I knew, would remain in my mind forever as one of the most unforgettable visions of the marine depths.

I went up to get my movie camera and continued my tour along the barrier. I was very deep and came upon a field of fire coral, over which I 'flew' safely. Then I rose a little to about sixty-five feet, right where the wall was perpendicular and the sun still indirect. I advanced in the shadow hoping to come upon a shark I could film.

A shark passed, but it was on the bottom, sixty-five feet from me and thirty from the surface. The water was so clear that I could see it sharply in the light that reached to the sandy bottom, along which the shark's shadow advanced.

Giorgio, a little distance away, experienced an exciting adventure which was a fitting end to our all too short dive at Zabargiadh. While I was shooting a scene with Vailati and Zecca, a shark was circling round us. We were dozens of yards deep, and when I finished my pictures of the two underwater men, I turned to see if I could get a good photo of the shark.

It was making a swift advance toward Giorgio's back. My friend was bent over with his eye on the Rolleiflex, photographing something ahead of him. The shark didn't seem to have any particularly warlike intentions. It went slowly above Giorgio and gradually decreased its speed. He was more curious than anything else. But it was a good twelve feet long, quite dark, and not a pleasant sight.

Suddenly its shadow covered Giorgio, who gave a start and surmised that something was right on top of him. He made a quick leap upward, and his head bumped against the shark's belly. The shark was so terrified that it disappeared in a flash from the scene.

Giorgio turned towards me, still frightened and startled. Fortunately we cannot speak under water, for on occasions like this we would not be able to find words to comment on such an incident. We took refuge in the silent language of the Blue Continent, grabbed each other's shoulders and spread open our arms. There couldn't have been a better comment.

From Zabargiadh to Cosseir it was a day and a night of sailing. My turn at the watch on deck occurred from midnight to four. How slowly can the night hours pass? I tried to cheat sleep by recalling the beautiful dive at Zabargiadh. Then Gigi appeared at my side.

'What time is it?' I asked.

'Three o'clock.'

'Still an hour to go.'

L*

Gigi had been doing his turn in the engine room and had come up on deck for a few moments in an effort to keep awake. We chatted to pass the time while the motor hummed monotonously. The *Formica* sailed up the Red Sea leaving in its wake a long tail of silver, a streak of phosphorescence which the propeller lit up beneath the water.

That evening the scientific group had made the first analysis of its collections and had drawn some conclusions. Gigi gave me a condensed picture of the results—very condensed because the full analysis and study will take two years and will be the work of many specialists. I have already talked about the most important general observations as we went along, but Gigi gave me a list of the collections. In the hold there were forty cases stacked away, with three hundred different species of fish in formalin (many unknown up to that time), plus many kinds of molluscs, thirty-five species of Coelenterata (madrepore and coral), fifteen perpheri (sponges), dozens of species of tunicates, worms, annelids, crustaceans, and a vast range of plankton caught in different localities.

At Cossier our Italian and Egyptian friends prepared great festivities for us and we passed the entire day telling tales to justify our changed appearance. Our faces were framed by beards and moustaches, and altogether we had lost a total of 350 pounds. These calculations were made by Silverio, who was upset about being the only one to return to Italy fatter. When they asked how in the world that happened, he answered evasively, but we all explained loudly that he was in charge of food supplies.

The next day we loaded our last provisions. We stopped for thirty-six hours at the shoals of the Ghifatin islands because of a damaged motor, and profited by shooting several good scenes of some tremendous jellyfish.

After the repairs, the *Formica's* fabulous speed of seven miles an hour was reduced to two and a half. We began to be worried

about catching the plane from Cairo on the twenty-seventh.
But the last long hours of the trip enabled us to draw up a tentative
score for the documentary group.

We filmed—within the limits of what was filmable—everything
that seemed interesting and useful for making a true and accurate
picture of the expedition's work, using seventy-five thousand
feet of coloured moving-picture film in the process. This film
will aid the expedition by showing the true nature of its work
and its results, and it will spread our concept of the Blue Continent throughout the world.

The vast series of still photographs taken during these months
may be used in the same way. Ravelli and I took about five
hundred pictures in colour and two thousand in black and white,
both under the water and above. Bucher, Roghi, Stuart, and
Priscilla were busy photographing as well, so I can only estimate
that the total will be about four thousand photographs.

I knew that when we returned home, we would rejoice in the
memory of the visions of unforgettable beauty we had seen and
be proud of having been among the few in the world to have
seen such wonders. Most of all, I will take deep satisfaction in
having worked to produce a visual documentation of that voyage,
which will let everyone share in those spectacles and adventures,
and experience some of our enthusiasm.

Two and a half miles an hour. The *Formica* didn't seem to
be moving at all. But ahead we saw the lights of Suez. Soon
we were on deck saying a last farewell to the Red Sea. We saw
the red beacon light of the canal, the beacon that had told us
five and a half months before that our adventure was beginning.
On 26 May, 1953, it announced that the adventure had ended.

The Supermaster rolled sweetly over the long runway, the
wheels drew up, and a hand seemed to pick us up and lift us
skyward. We crossed the labyrinth of the Nile, which soon
faded in the distance, then left the coast and flew over the sea.

Finally, high in the sky, we were surrounded only by the infinite blue above and the darker blue below—just the same as when we left the surface and descended deeper and deeper into the blue of the Blue Continent.

The roar of the motors repeats the name: Blue Continent, Blue Continent. Will man always be in flight toward new conquests? The last small piece of conquered land, the top of Mount Everest, is now ours. In the search for new worlds, some think of the moon and Mars. Why don't they think of the Blue Continent, so vast, so rich, so near at hand?

The earth swarms with inhabitants—millions more every year. The earth hungers and seems doomed to more hunger as populations increase much faster than food production possibly can. To-day we are 2.2 billion people. If we continue to increase with the same speed, we shall be three billion in the year 2000.

But there are still hundreds of thousands of acres on the earth ready and capable of being cultivated. The Sahara? The Mato Grosso? All right, but there is more land than all that—rich land for crops of all kinds—lying close to most of us, beneath a little beautiful blue water. The Blue Continent can end the spectre of starvation and want throughout the world. The first explorers have penetrated its borders and learned something about it. Let us hope that many more will follow.

Appendix

Underwater Photography
by Folco Quilici and Giorgio Ravelli

To-day, the movie camera plays a strategic part in every expedition. The immediacy of the picture helps the camera to popularise and publicise the aims of an expedition, its adventures and its results.

Our ambition was to wring from the sea the secrets and mysteries of its depths, its life, its colours and lights. We wanted to produce an image powerful enough to satisfy those who had heard the enthusiastic accounts of our adventures. We wanted photographs and films which would whet the curiosity of those who were not yet aware of the secrets of this new sport. We wanted to make enthusiasts of those who were still sceptical as to the emotions which such a strange and fantastic exploration could evoke.

The Camera: As a rule, the camera is equipped with certain special features, and in using it, certain specific and sometimes quite complex factors have to be kept in mind.

By 'complex' we do not mean those terribly complicated underwater gadgets sometimes shown in technical magazines. Not the sort of brain storms represented, for instance, by a cage with watertight walls, capable of carrying two men, both comfortably stretched out on a small rubber mattress, one operating a movie camera, the other a still camera, with plenty of additional space for lamps, accumulators, supplies, air bottles, dynamos, etc. This gadget was warmly recommended in the columns of a widespread monthly by someone who has obviously never seen the sea. Our task was more difficult than the designing of gadgets abounding in clever 'inventions'.

We were concerned, really, with achieving the utmost simplicity, without sacrificing an ounce of technical perfection, for all those instruments which had to be locked in protective containers and lowered into the sea. Under water, the simplest mechanisms net the best results. We often used old iron boxes, parts of water taps, bits of gear taken from grandfather clocks, and other materials patiently collected from secondhand dealers.

Actually, we had to reconcile two purposes: the goal of simplicity on the one hand; on the other the technical requirements of colour and monochrome photography, with and without artificial lighting, plus problems peculiar to the underwater colour movie. These two different objectives, however, had a common determinator: that of practical usefulness.

The cameras we used for making movies were two Kodak Specials with spring drive and two lenses; and for the stills a Rolleiflex in which an additional lens could be used for shots up to one foot. The use of the spring drive should be emphasised. We chose it deliberately in preference to an electric motor because the latter involves the problem of cooling off, as well as the problem of special batteries. These cameras were lowered into the sea wrapped in special metal cases, the walls of which were 1/8th of an inch thick.

Figure 1, the cross section of the watertight fastening that was used, shows one of the four rods attached to the sides of the lid to allow for a rapid opening or closing. By giving the nut a few twists and turning the rod, the lid can be removed.

The containers were relatively heavy. As far as the Rolleiflex was concerned, this somewhat facilitated the underwater work. In the case of the Kodak cameras, some weight was eliminated for underwater operation by means of wooden wings about 3 feet in length, which served to stabilise their movements.

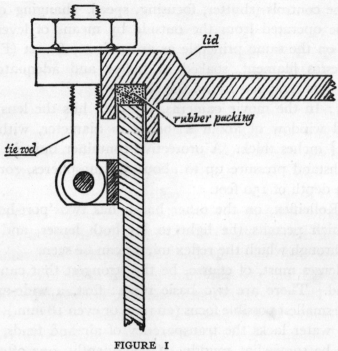

FIGURE I

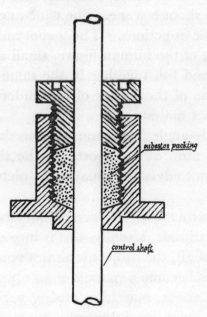

FIGURE 2

All the controls (shutter, focusing, speed, changing of lenses) could be operated from the outside by means of levers which worked on the same principle as an ordinary faucet (Figure 2). An asbestos filament, soaked in tallow and adequately compressed, was wrapped round the shaft.

Lenses: In the movie cameras, the light hits the lens through a round window of about 2 inches in diameter, with a pane about 1½ inches thick. A protective container built in this way can withstand pressure up to about 5 atmospheres, corresponding to a depth of 150 feet.

The Rolleiflex, on the other hand, has two 'port-holes', one oval which permits the light to hit both lenses, and another round through which the reflex mirror can be seen.

The lenses must, of course, be the strongest that can possibly be found. There are two basic types: first, a wide-angle lens with the smallest possible focus (20 mm. or even 18 mm.), required because water lacks the transparency of air and tends, in addition, to be somewhat muddy. Consequently, one often has to get pretty close to shoot a scene. The wide-angle lens, moreover, has certain specific functions. The panoramic view of a submarine landscape, of the human figure, small against Cyclopæan scenery; of men and fish together in the same picture, recreates on the screen some of the poetry of the underwater world, conveying a sense of its majesty.

Besides the wide-angle lens, one also needs a telephoto lens of 50 mm. to 75 mm. at the most, for the shooting of details. Larger lenses are not advisable because the picture would become unsteady.

Operating the Camera: Only in exceptional cases can the camera be mounted on a tripod. Usually, this is impossible for a variety of reasons. First of all, the subject is almost constantly in motion, so that most scenes become a pursuit of an object by an operator, who has to roam about, searching among various views for one that promises to make an interesting picture. Obviously, he cannot have an assistant swim after him to put down a tripod whenever there is a chance for a nice picture. Besides, by the time the camera is installed on the tripod, the object may have moved on several hundred yards farther. Those real-life, under-water actors are unfortunately rather undisciplined and not good at taking orders. And what about taking a scene near the surface, while the floor is seventy-five feet below and might be covered with a vast undergrowth. The tripod would need rather outsized legs. In short, one has to keep moving.

Assuming, however, that the cameraman is an excellent swimmer; that he feels perfectly at home under water; and that he knows how to use his respiratory gear so that he will always be in perfect balance (i.e., that he neither goes up toward the surface, nor sinks when he wishes to remain in one spot), there still remains the problem of the movie camera, which is in itself extremely heavy. With the added weight of the container box, which is of wrought bronze, it would seem an impossibility to maintain a desired position without support, grasp the camera with both hands, and at the same time turn it to the left or right. Actually, it can be done because the designer, when planning the underwater container box, calculated the exact relation between its weight and the volume at which it will stay in balance, so that it can 'float' without weight. Thus, even a camera of gigantic dimensions can be handled without trouble by a swimming cameraman. The 'wings' of the camera, of course, aid immensely in stabilising it.

Lighting: It is usually assumed that only a small amount of light penetrates below the water. This assumption is quite wrong, especially for the area in which most of the filming is done, i.e., from zero to 120 feet. Even at a depth of 180 feet, scenes have been shot with excellent results. The fact is that there is light under water—a different light, to be sure, from that which we experience above the surface, but nevertheless sufficient. The diver finds himself enveloped by a strong, diffused glow which reaches him partly from the surface, and is partly reflected from the layers of sand covering the floor. *The exposure should be adjusted, by and large, on the rule that the lens must be opened two stops directly below the surface; and one additional stop for approximately each additional 24 feet of depth.* Practically speaking, if the lens is open at 16 outside the water, you would have to set it at 8 for the first 24 feet; at 5:6 from 25 to 48 feet; at 4:5 from 48 to 72—and so on. As one approaches the floor, the exposure has to be adjusted according to different rules because, as was mentioned, the sand covering the floor reflects a great deal of light.

The following table suggests the exposures under which we reached most satisfactory results for still shots:

TABLE I

STOP NUMBERS FOR NATURAL LIGHT

	Depth in feet	0-6	15	30	60	90
Monochrome black & white 21° *DIN* (*80 Weston*) *1/50 sec.*	Clear water or with dark background	8	6.3	5.6	4	3.5
	White background at a distance of 15 ft.	9	8	—	—	—
	30 ft.	8	6.3	6.3	—	—
	60 ft.	8	6.3	5.6	5.6	—
Ansco Colour 1/50 sec. Ektachrome	Dark objects	3.5	2.8	—	—	—
	Bright objects	4.5	3.5	—	—	—

It is even possible to take pictures inside an underwater cave. In this case, the camera has to be turned against the entrance; or, in other words, towards the bright area contrasting with the dark shapes of the surrounding rock. The lens is adjusted in accordance with the light, and you are ready for shooting. In these surroundings, all shapes are reduced to black silhouettes moving against a bright background. This again is a peculiar effect high-lighting the underwater atmosphere. One obtains the identical effect by photographing against the light, with the camera turned upward, toward the surface. The lens is stopped down, and once more the figures appear as silhouettes. The picture achieves a particularly suggestive effect of depth, if the figures are moving either downward or upward. This creates the fantastic impression of flight—which man does indeed experience in exploring the submarine world.

Normally, the camera stays at approximately the same level as the object. Shooting from above is definitely inadvisable, because the picture looks squashed and so fails to convey any sense of the actual depth. The following exposure table for a movie camera within twenty-four feet of the surface and in bright sunlight may help clarify some of these relationships:

TABLE II

I: Object on sandy or rocky ground; bright:	f. 6.3
dark:	4.5
II: Panoramic view with blue sea in background:	5.6
III: From above, against bright background:	5.6
against dark background:	4
IV: From below the object—diagonal:	8
vertical:	11
vertical, fully against the sun:	16

The problem of artificial lighting and colour: On a sunny day, one may take colour shots under water without the help of artificial lighting. In *theory*, shots can be taken to a depth of seventy-five feet without too much under-exposure. However, below fifteen feet, shooting colour film is no longer a problem of the quantity of available light; another element enters in.

163

Under the impact of sunlight, sea water behaves like a bluish green filter. Red and purple radiations are absorbed with an increasing intensity according to the quantity of water extending between the object and the source of light.

At a few feet depth, red colours disappear completely; and as one descends farther, also orange and yellow, until everything assumes a uniform grey-green tone.

Artificial lighting is required—much like the flash bulb for a night picture—to make the floor of the sea reveal the wealth of colours hidden beneath the blue-green blanket of the water. For a variety of reasons, all connected with the fact that under-water movies approximate the conditions of real-life documentaries rather than the filming of a staged scene, artificial lighting is a fairly complex proposition.

For black and white photography this is, of course, irrelevant. But for colour photography, it poses a problem of primary importance. At a depth of thirty feet a colour photograph will turn out totally blue. It does not help to employ coloured filters, because of the almost total absence of radiations for the colours one desires to stress.

In moderate depths such as six to fifteen feet, the layer of water is still thin enough to behave as a very light filter. Hence, one can obtain good results without employing specific devices.

By holding a source of light near the object one achieves the double advantage of augmenting the actual lighting and of obtaining a practically white-light effect while the entire mass of water above is no longer of importance. The only way to reveal those colours which the human eye is unable to see under water is by the use of artificial-lighting devices, especially those equipped with a flash lamp.

The handful of professional underwater photographers is divided into two distinct schools: those who insist upon using electronic flash lamps and those who are obsessed with a passion for using the magnesium flash bulb. Both methods have advantages and disadvantages, but we have found that the electronic flash lamp is less suited for routine work because of its complicated design and the danger of high tension inherent in its use.

The flash-bulb lamp is quite easy to build. It simply consists of a container shaped like a tube which holds three batteries of 1.5 volts each. The container is attached to a lamp socket, the electric contacts of which are immersed in the water, and there is a fixture in which to insert the reflector. The reflector should be of first-rate design because the effective lighting of the whole scene depends entirely on its presence. If the lamp floated freely in water, a mere five per cent of the emitting light would strike the object. The reflector makes possible a utilisation up to sixty per cent.

To build a flash lamp according to this design requires very little effort and negligible cost. On the other hand, operating expenses are rather high. By contrast, the electronic flash lamp requires great initial costs and cumbersome construction—a cylinder of eight inches in diameter and six feet in length, according to Rebikoff's design—while the operating expenses are slight.

Table III lists the data for satisfactory exposure with colour films, based on our own experience.

TABLE III

GE 22 lamp—1/50 sec. ansco colour—Agfacolour

Distance in feet		$1\frac{1}{2}$	3	6	9
Depth 6-30 ft.	Bright objects	6.3	5.6	4	3.5
	Dark objects	4.5	4	3.5	2.8
Depth 30-90 ft.	Bright objects	5.5	4	3.5	2.8
	Dark objects	4	3.5	2.8	—
In the dark.	Bright objects	4	3.5	2.8	—
	Dark objects	3.5	2.8	—	—

If one wants to take objects at a considerable distance in effective light, one may use a lamp which allows the lighting of two flashes at the same time, one of the regular type, and one of the blue-colour type. While the first serves to heighten the colours of relatively close objects, the second lights up more distant scenes with sufficient intensity.

Two of the photographs in this book, taken with and without flash lamps, have been juxtaposed for comparison. They reveal the miraculous capacity of the flash lamp to bring to life colours which the eye is unable to perceive.

It should be noted that the intensity of light, capable of producing the colour tones seen in the pictures in this book, which have been taken with the flash lamp, would require at least ten lamps of 5000 watts, concentrated on an area of not more than thirty square feet. Obviously this gear would be too cumbersome to handle.

For our own shots—such a battery of searchlights being out of the question—we insisted on having enough light to penetrate the bluish mist which was always spreading across the picture. After we had studied the problem for some time, we decided to set up small clusters of four lamps, each of 1000 watts with a reflector, mounted on discs and connected with the surface by watertight electric wire about ninety feet long. Each disc had a handle, so that a man swimming close to the camera was able to hold one disc in each hand—a total of eight lamps, or 8000 watts.

With four men, we were able to obtain a lighting up to 32,000 watts. Actually, this still was not enough, but we let it go at that. The lights were, in this way, concentrated on some detail such as a high-coloured background, coral, a halcyon, some floating algae. The backdrop stood out so from the rest that its different levels became sufficiently evident to give the proper depth to the picture. Sometimes we would obtain interesting stereoscopic effects. If we wanted to shoot details or coloured objects a few feet below the surface, our searchlight battery proved to be more than sufficient.

Special Effects: Long-standing experience in underwater films has taught us the use of certain special effects.

So far, nobody has been able to take pictures in backward motion. While it is easy to swim forward, pushing the camera ahead of oneself and thereby keeping it steady, this is definitely impossible under water during backward strokes. The following methods have been tried by us—usually with success:

One: Reverse Gear Method. Advancing with the camera in reverse gear. In projecting the picture upon the screen, it will have to be upside down, so that the motion remains in reverse. The only thing to avoid is having any fish or human being on the scene, because they will appear to be moving backward.

Two: 'Rod' Method. The underwater container box is equipped with a rod, held in horizontal position. This may be attached to the wing. To get a good picture, the cameraman first has to check the distance between camera and object. Next, he starts the camera, and as soon as that is done, lifts himself up behind it. Two men start advancing at both ends of the rod, pushing the camera backward, taking care that the fins do not enter the picture. The effect is quite good although the procedure is cumbersome. However, the scene may easily look wobbly on the screen.

Three: 'Flight' Method. This is by all means the best and most successful of the three. The camera, as mentioned before, is equipped with 'wings' enabling it to float, without rising or sinking when left to itself. However, in this method, one loads the back part of the container with a small weight. Close to a sandy point, one allows the camera to sink. It will descend in a sloping curve, completing an automatic backward swim.

A man who has to be filmed while descending under water should think only of staying constantly within the frame of the lens, so that his figure remains on the optical axis. The result will be an excellent picture of descent from surface to floor. If the film starts exactly below the surface, exposure should be adjusted according to the light in that area. As one descends, the scene becomes gradually somewhat under-exposed. But that is perfectly all right, since it conveys the feeling of diving.

There is another special effect particularly suitable for hunting scenes. To increase the inherent excitement and to help the audience share in the spirit of a fight with the inhabitants of the sea—in short, to produce a maximum impact, we equipped one of the three cameras we used in the Red Sea with an underwater gun, to be attached to the side of the camera by four simple hooks. The gun pushes out so that it is always in the field of vision. The right hand grasps the handle of the camera, with the forefinger on the starter. With the left hand one holds the other handle of the camera, and the forefinger rests on the trigger of the gun. This makes it possible to sight, and at the same time pursue, a nice specimen of fish, take aim and fire. Nine out of ten times, the result will be startling and dramatic.

But we ought to add that even the combination of the most perfect technical mastery and the best underwater swimming are not sufficient to produce underwater movies of real documentary value. One other element has to be considered—a thorough familiarity with the habits, the weaknesses, the cunning of the inhabitants of the sea. One has to know that it is advisable to remain still in front of some fish; that one has to tease the cernia; that one should make metallic noises to arouse the curiosity of the silver mullet; that photographing sea eels requires the patience of a saint; that, in front of polyps, one must remain motionless or wave some white object; that rays should not be annoyed by any movement until they are safely grounded on the sea floor, but that one must pursue hard on their heels as soon as they rise for a 'flight'. In short, one needs a long-standing experience, which naturally can be acquired only through practice.

When we arrived at the Red Sea, for some time we were at our wits' end. How should we behave with certain types of fish which we had never seen until then? We were especially worried about the bolder ones because we did not know how to approach them. The sharks and the barracudas, in particular, were our undoing. As soon as we saw one, we would paddle after it, but the big fish would notice us in a flash. We learned eventually that those 'wild' fishes would come toward us when we proceeded into the open sea but would turn to escape as soon as we came closer. We began to exploit that discovery. In the end, feigning a retreat at their approach, we managed to film some extremely close encounters with these fishes. The shark or the barracuda would be emboldened and start diving after us. We would continue our flight. The fish would come still closer. When the fish was really at close range, we would start the camera, taking him by surprise. In this way, we were able to get very interesting close-ups. Perhaps this sounds like a somewhat sensational method, but risk and adventure are part of the job.

All these are not just theoretical assertions. They are, rather, the result of long-standing experience in underwater movie-making. Perhaps these few observations will help those who might be planning some similar venture.

And thus, we come back to the general subject of this book— the opportunities awaiting man on the 'Blue Continent'. To underline once again the great challenge which this new frontier presents might be the most fitting conclusion for these remarks. The submarine world opens up new frontiers for the scientific, popular and—why not?—adventure type of film. The stage is set, on the floor of the sea, for any team ready to descend.